The
Pura
Belpré
Awards

Celebrating Latino
Authors and Illustrators

Edited by Rose Zertuche Treviño

The Association for Library Service to Children

REFORMA, National Association to Promote Library
and Information Services to Latinos and the Spanish-Speaking

AMERICAN LIBRARY ASSOCIATION

Chicago   2006

While extensive effort has gone into ensuring the reliability of information appearing in this book, the publisher makes no warranty, express or implied, on the accuracy or reliability of the information, and does not assume and hereby disclaims any liability to any person for any loss or damage caused by errors or omissions in this publication.

Design and composition by ALA Editions in Janson Text and Zapf Chancery using QuarkXPress 5.0 on a PC platform

Printed on 50-pound white offset, a pH-neutral stock, and bound in 10-point cover stock by McNaughton & Gunn

Cover image from *Just a Minute*, by Yuyi Morales, courtesy of Chronicle Books.

Photo of Pura Belpré on page xi from the Pura Belpré Papers, Archives of the Puerto Rican Diaspora, Centro de Estudios Puertorriqueños, Hunter College, City University of New York.

Illustrations following page 16 used by permission. Credit information appears on page 81.

The paper used in this publication meets the minimum requirements of American National Standard for Information Sciences—Permanence of Paper for Printed Library Materials, ANSI Z39.48-1992. ∞

Library of Congress Cataloging-in-Publication Data

The Pura Belpré Awards : celebrating Latino authors and illustrators / Rose Zertuche Treviño, editor.
    p. cm.
    Includes bibliographical references and index.
    ISBN 0-8389-3562-1
    1. Belpre Medal—Bio-bibliography. 2. American literature—Hispanic American authors—Awards. 3. Children's literature, American—Awards. 4. Picture books for children—Awards—United States. 5. Children—Books and reading—United States. 6. Hispanic Americans in literature—Bibliography. 7. Hispanic American authors—Biography. 8. Hispanic American illustrators—Biography. I. Treviño, Rose Zertuche.
    Z1037.A2P87 2006
    810.9'9282079—dc22[B]   2005037628

ISBN-10: 0-8389-3562-1
ISBN-13: 978-0-8389-3562-0

Printed in the United States of America.

10   09   08   07   06   5   4   3   2   1

CONTENTS

ILLUSTRATIONS

PREFACE

*T*reasures can be found where you least expect them. For those of us who love the written word, those treasures are books. Within the pages of a book, one can truly lose oneself and escape to the world created by the writer, a world of make-believe, a world rich with culture, a world with traditions so different and yet also so similar to our own. The Pura Belpré Award celebrates such treasures created by Latino authors and illustrators.

If you have heard of the Pura Belpré Award, you know that it is a relatively new award presented biennially and cosponsored by the National Association to Promote Library and Information Services to Latinos and the Spanish-Speaking (REFORMA) and the Association for Library Service to Children (ALSC). If you have not heard of the award, you may have difficulty pronouncing its name, so here is a little help: Pura (POOH rah) Belpré (bell PREH).

So you are not of Latin heritage—it doesn't matter. This award is to be embraced by all who value children's literature, for children absorb what we give them, children love what we teach them to love, and children value what we show them has merit. And so the chapters are written, one Latino voice at a time, and you are cordially invited to read the books, savor the illustrations, and then simply enjoy what the award-winning authors and illustrators have given us.

Sincerely,
The Pura Belpré Awards Bookwriting team

Rose Zertuche Treviño, editor
Sandra Rios Balderrama
Oralia Garza de Cortés
Jean Hatfield
Ana-Elba Pavon

ACKNOWLEDGMENTS

*D*reams begin with a simple thought. When pursued, dreams can become reality. You now hold a dream first conceived by two librarians, Oralia Garza de Cortés and Sandra Rios Balderrama, who believed that it was worth acknowledging the work of Latinos in books for children. It is through their joint perseverance that the Pura Belpré Award was established in 1996 and is presented biennially to a Latino writer and illustrator whose work best portrays, affirms, and celebrates the Latino cultural experience in an outstanding work of literature for children and youth. Their vision brought us this award, which allows talented Latino writers and illustrators to shine. Thanks to this award, readers of all ages have been introduced to a culture rich in tradition, where *familia* is important and *la cultura* must be passed on to new generations.

Also to be acknowledged are the other two writers who contributed to this book, Jean Hatfield and Ana-Elba Pavon. As past Belpré committee members, they too possess the passion to promote the award and thereby give it continued visibility.

Laura Schulte-Cooper, program officer of communications for ALSC, has been of invaluable assistance from the very beginning of this writing venture. Thanks also go to all who have served on the Pura Belpré Award Committee. Through their work, this award has continued to gain merit in the eyes of librarians, educators, publishers, authors, and illustrators. Finally, thank you to the two sponsoring groups, REFORMA and ALSC, for embracing the dream and giving the award the national recognition needed to convey that Latino writers and illustrators have much to share and much to be appreciated by all readers.

Rose Zertuche Treviño

INTRODUCTION

WHO WAS PURA BELPRÉ?

Oralia Garza de Cortés

Pura Teresa Belpré, beloved author, prolific storyteller, children's librarian par excellence, folklorist, puppeteer, and people's advocate, was born in 1899, in Cidra, Puerto Rico, where she spent her childhood and formative years. She moved to New York City in 1920 and shortly thereafter was hired by the New York Public Library as an assistant librarian at the 135th Street Branch in Harlem. Belpré pioneered bilingual story-times and cultural programming as a way to reach out to the city's growing Puerto Rican community.

Shortly after starting the cultural programming, she enrolled in the New York Public Library's own library school. Because Belpré was raised in a culture rich in oral storytelling tradition, she quickly mastered the storytelling class taught by Mary Gould Davis. (Belpré's well-known version of *Pérez and Martina*, first published in 1932, was originally written and presented as part of her storytelling coursework.) In the following years, Belpré developed a reputation as a skilled and talented storyteller. She also worked closely with Puerto Rican community-based organizations, telling her beloved folkloric stories to the first wave of Puerto Rican immigrants who arrived in New York in search of jobs shortly after Puerto Rico gained independence from Spain.

In 1943 Belpré married Clarence Cameron White, a renowned African American violinist and composer, who was then considered to be America's premier musician. Belpré left the New York Public Library to accompany White on his national and international tours. Belpré then began writing and publishing the folktales that she had told as a children's librarian, fulfilling a promise she had made to Mary Gould Davis that she would work to make these stories become part of New York Public Library's permanent collection.

Pérez and Martina, the popular folktale long considered a classic of Hispanic children's literature and known in many versions throughout the Americas, soon became a classic of American children's literature as well. In 2000 Belpré's version was named one of the one hundred best children's books of the twentieth century by the New York Public Library. Thanks to collaborative efforts between REFORMA and Books on Demand, her version returned to print in 2005 after a thirty-eight-year hiatus.

Belpré's *The Tiger and the Rabbit and Other Tales* (Houghton Mifflin, 1946) became the first collection of Puerto Rican folktales published in the United States. Belpré authored a total of eight books for children, including *Santiago*, a picture book reflective of modern Puerto Rican children's experiences living in New York. Belpré's memories of an idyllic childhood spent in Puerto Rico are the basis for her first and only novel for older children, *Firefly Summer*, which she wrote during World War II. The novel was published posthumously by Arte Público Press as part of its Recovering the U.S. Hispanic Literary Heritage series.

Belpré also translated fifteen children's books from English into Spanish, including *The Legend of Our Lady of Guadalupe* (Holiday House, 1980). It remains in print to this day.

After the death of her husband in 1960, Belpré returned to New York City and to the New York Public Library to continue her work, shaping and influencing children's services by providing culturally relevant programming for both children and families. From 1968 to 1978 Belpré worked with Lillian Lopez on the South Bronx Library Project, a Title I project funded by the Library Services and Construction Act (LSCA). The project aimed to provide comprehensive services to nine branches with increasing numbers of Spanish-speaking patrons. In addition to programs and services, the project also focused on collection development and bibliography. With Mary K. Conwell, Belpré and Lopez developed a comprehensive annotated bibliography of books in Spanish, *Libros en Español*, for the New York Public Library in 1971.

Belpré died July 1, 1982, the day after the Coordinator's Council of the New York Public Library honored her for her service to the library.

Sources

"Biographical Sketch." In the Pura Belpré Papers Finding Aid. Archives of the Centro de Estudios Puertorriqueños, Hunter College, City University of New York. http://centropr.org/lib-arc/belpre.html.

Gonzalez, Lisa Sanchez. "Pura Belpré: The Children's Ambassador." In *Latina Legacies: Identity, Biography, and Community*, edited by Vicki L. Ruiz and Virginia Sánchez Korrol. New York: Oxford University Press, 2005.

Lopez, Lillian, with Pura Belpré. "Reminiscences of Two Turned-On Librarians." In *Puerto Rican Perspectives*, edited and with an introduction by Edward Mapp. Metuchen, NJ: Scarecrow Press, 1974.

Hernandez-Delgado, Julio I. "Pura Teresa Belpré, Storyteller and Pioneer Puerto Rican Librarian." *Library Quarterly* 62, no. 4 (October 1992): 425–40.

Books Written by Pura Belpré

Pérez and Martina: A Portorican Folk Tale. Illustrated by Carlos Sánchez. New York: Frederick Warne, 1932, 1960.

Pérez and Martina: A Puerto Rican Folktale. Illustrated by Carlos Sánchez. New York: Viking, 1961.

Juan Bobo and the Queen's Necklace: A Puerto Rican Folk Tale. Illustrated by Christine Price. New York: Frederick Warne, 1962.

The Tiger and the Rabbit and Other Tales. Illustrated by Tomie de Paola. Philadelphia: Lippincott, 1965.

Pérez and Martina. Read by the author. New York: CMS, 1966. 12-inch LP, 33⅓ rpm.

Santiago. Illustrated by Symeon Shimin. New York: Frederick Warne, 1966.

OTÉ: A Puerto Rican Folktale. Illustrated by Paul Galdone. New York: Pantheon, 1969.

OTÉ: Un cuento folklorico puertorriqueños. New York: Pantheon, 1969.

Once in Puerto Rico. Illustrated by Christine Price. New York: Frederick Warne, 1973.

The Rainbow-Colored Horse. Illustrated by Antonio Martorell. New York: Frederick Warne, 1978.

Firefly Summer. Houston, TX: Piñata Books, 1996.

BIRTH OF THE AWARD

Sandra Rios Balderrama

The Pura Belpré Award began with the simple introduction of two Latina children's librarians, both of Mexican heritage. Oralia Garza de Cortés and Sandra Rios Balderrama met at the 1986 American Library Association (ALA) Annual Conference in San Francisco. The introduction led to honest conversations between the two about the delivery of—or lack of—quality library services to Latino children and families throughout the United States. Garza de Cortés and Rios Balderrama, in Texas and California, respectively, had created their own tools for service. They had compiled their own collections of *rimas y canciones*, learned the guitar chords to songs by the great children's composer and singer José-Luis Orozco, and followed the oral tradition of storytelling by learning folktales from Latin American countries and the Caribbean. Still, mothers would ask Garza de Cortés for books that pictured Latino children, and Rios Balderrama needed picture books for her bilingual preschool hours and entertaining children's fiction for her book clubs and class visits. Accountability to their patrons' requests and needs was foremost in both of their minds. Books with diverse imagery and portrayals of the Latino child's experience were desperately needed to fulfill the library's accountability to Latino patrons and to make the library accessible to a broader public.

Soon Garza de Cortés and Rios Balderrama began speaking seriously about the possibility of an award for Latino children's literature. In the course of their ongoing dialogue, both librarians realized that Latino authors and illustrators were also needed—to write the books. They were well aware of the argument that any truly good writer could write about any cultural experience. Their intent was not to argue this point but to ensure that Latinos were among the pool of truly good writers to be recognized and published. The African American library community had claimed their own documentation, creation, and illustration with the Coretta Scott King Award, and this was a profound source of inspiration to Garza de Cortés and Rios Balderrama. Their conversations gave way to a promise of commitment and action to create a children's literature award that would honor Latino authors and illustrators and ultimately affirm the diverse experiences of Latino children.

After deciding that the future of this particular award needed a shared home, Garza de Cortés and Rios Balderrama began discussions with key leaders from REFORMA and ALSC. Linda Perkins, former president of ALSC, was particularly instrumental in facilitating the idea among her ALSC colleagues. While the process of award establishment was under way, Toni Bissessar, a Latina librarian of Puerto Rican heritage and member of both associations, suggested that the award be named in honor of Pura Belpré. The legacy of Ms. Belpré, the first Latina librarian at the New York Public Library, became the touchstone for the founders' tenacity, perseverance, accountability, and inspiration.

Eleven years passed before the first award was given in 1996, but Garza de Cortés and Rios Balderrama now celebrate the inclusion of the Latino experience in children's books.

THE PARTNERSHIP

Sandra Rios Balderrama and Oralia Garza de Cortés

When the idea for a Latino children's book award was first considered, key concerns were access and visibility. How were children to find quality books written by someone of their own heritage? How were parents, librarians, and classroom teachers to know about these books and promote them? How would information about the award be disseminated among librarians and to schools and libraries around the country?

The key organizers in the award's establishment, Oralia Garza de Cortés and Sandra Rios Balderrama, pondered the feasibility of a joint award. Both were members of ALSC and REFORMA. The two organizations together, they felt, could make a difference in promoting this important Latino children's literature award. Although ALSC provided the best book evaluation and training, REFORMA provided the connection to the Latino community and the expertise in cultural content. Together, the two organizations could create a children's book award that centered on authentic Latino cultural experiences and would be recognized by the whole of the library world as well as by the publishing industry. Through collaborative partnership, ALSC and REFORMA each could draw upon the resources and strengths that the other organization brought to the table.

But the Belpré Award also needed the recognition and visibility that the Caldecott Medal, Newbery Medal, and Coretta Scott King Award enjoyed. During this period, Garza de Cortés was beginning to develop her reputation as an outspoken advocate for library services for Latino children. She had just been elected to the ALSC Board of Directors; her three-year tenure would give her time to take action. Rios Balderrama, on the other hand, was skilled in managing group processes and in relationship and coalition building, and she was a skilled negotiator.

During this period, Linda Perkins, a former colleague and friend of Rios Balderrama, was serving her term as president of ALSC. Rios Balderrama approached Perkins about a potential partnership and received a strong, positive response. Rios Balderrama invited Perkins to help REFORMA shape the conversations about developing a quality children's award, which led to the development of the terms and criteria for the award. Perkins became the first ALSC president to attend a REFORMA board meeting, and both Garza de Cortés and Rios Balderrama became familiar faces at ALSC board meetings and events.

Once the terms and criteria were developed, the boards of directors for both REFORMA and ALSC were approached. Motions to establish the award were set in place and paved the way for the discussion and final approval of the Pura Belpré Award as a joint award of ALSC and REFORMA.

In 1996 the award was formally established. Both boards immediately went to work to appoint a joint jury, and the first author and illustrator awards were given at the First National REFORMA Conference held in Austin, Texas, in August 1996.

CELEBRACIÓN

On a hot and sultry afternoon in Orlando, Florida, magic came to visit. It entered the Rosen Plaza Hotel and stayed for two whole hours. The event was the 2004 Pura Belpré Award Ceremony, or *Celebración*, and attendees were in for a treat. The young dancers from the Salsa Heat Dance Company, who had the crowd cheering as they shared their energetic dance moves, marked just the beginning.

The awards portion of the event soon began, and the first recipient of the Illustrator Honor Award—for *First Day in Grapes*, written by L. King Pérez—was called to the podium. So overcome with emotion was illustrator Robert Casilla that he was speechless for a moment. David Diaz, a Caldecott Medal winner, was next to accept an Illustrator Honor Award—for *The Pot That Juan Built*, written by Nancy Andrews-Goebel. A true charmer, he graciously accepted his award, choosing to leave the limelight for the new awardees.

If anyone in the audience had ever wondered what it is like to be in a foreign country with little command of the language, Yuyi Morales let them know that feeling. She opened her heart and soul and left hardly a dry eye in the room. To hear her speak was such a joy as she accepted both an Illustrator Honor Award for *Harvesting Hope: The Story of César Chávez*, written by Kathleen Krull, and the Illustrator Award for *Just a Minute: A Trickster Tale and Counting Book*.

Next came Nancy Osa, who accepted an Author Honor Award for her first novel, *Cuba 15*. By reaching out to her Cuban heritage, Osa connected with her fifteen-year-old character, Violet Paz. The night also included a love story—between Amada Irma Pérez and her family, who were in attendance and cheering for her as she accepted her Author Honor Award for *My Diary from Here to There / Mi diario de aquí hasta allá*.

In the final award presentation, Julia Alvarez gave a touching acceptance for her Author Award–winning book, *Before We Were Free*. Her speech was everything and more, both grand and simple. She then shared with the mesmerized crowd a poem she had written just for librarians.

At the close of the event, all attendees joined hands or locked arms and began to sway and sing along with José-Luis Orozco's rendition of *De colores*. Although unable to attend, Orozco had willingly given permission for his song to be played at the ceremony. What a grand finish to an enchanting afternoon. Those who attended were rewarded and charmed. Those who did not, missed out.

But the *Celebración* is held every two years, and magic is sure to return each time as this award, given to a Latino writer and illustrator whose work best portrays, affirms, and celebrates the Latino cultural experience in an outstanding work of literature for children and youth, continues to celebrate the Latino heritage.

Part I

Author Awards

2006
MEDAL WINNER

Canales, Viola. *The Tequila Worm*. New York: Wendy Lamb Books, 2005.

Doña Clara could conjure up the most amazing stories and, according to her, young Sofia had inherited her great-great-grandmother's gift for mule-kicking. Welcome to the barrio in McAllen, Texas, where Sofia's world is rich with strong family ties and Mexican cultural traditions. It's a world in which religious beliefs blend with celebrations such as Day of the Dead. Here, Easter is a time for *cascarones*, the traditional eggshells filled with confetti, which offer an opportunity for Papa to bring out his guitar and sing *De Colores*.

When Sofia wins a scholarship to an elite boarding school in Austin, her family experiences mixed feelings. They want the best for Sofia, but they worry about her moving away from home and away from the culture that has been her life. At the school, Sofia is suddenly thrust into a world of privileged kids—some who accept her and others who do not. Sofia tentatively enters this world with dreams for herself; and when she is homesick, it is time to eat the tequila worm.

From *The Tequila Worm*, by Viola Canales

I missed my room altar, especially at night, when I thought of home most. I liked looking at the glow-in-the-dark rosary and remembering my last birthday. I especially missed Lucy and hearing her giggle at the crazy stories I told her before going off to sleep.

HONOR

Bernier-Grand, Carmen T. *César: ¡Sí, Se Puede! Yes, We Can!* Illustrated by
David Diaz. New York: Marshall Cavendish, 2004.

Bernier-Grand's series of free-verse poems depict significant milestones in the
life of César Chávez. From Chávez's hopeful beginnings in Yuma, Arizona, to
his hard-scrabble existence as a *campesino* in the fields of California, Bernier-
Grand highlights the impetus for Chávez's passionate advocacy of the rights of
farm workers. She provides an overview of his political activism and its impact.
The poems are simple but evocative in their exploration of Chávez's life. They
incorporate his words, which add immediacy to the message. In "Don't
Mourn—Organize!" the author expands on Chávez's statement "If you don't
read new books, / You are left behind. / I spend time reading into the night. /
I want to be ahead of others." Bernier-Grand shows us Chávez's drive and ded-
ication to the cause with simple but effective words. This exploration of his life
goes beyond the typical biography to provide an artful insight into one of
America's heroes. The author includes a glossary, a chronology, source notes,
and significant quotations from Chávez's writings.

From *¡Sí, Se Puede! Yes, We Can!*
by Carmen T. Bernier-Grand

Who could tell
that Cesario Estrada Chávez,
the shy American
wearing a checkered shirt,
walking with a cane to ease his back
from the burden of the fields,
could organize so many people
to march for *La Causa*, The Cause?

Mora, Pat. *Doña Flor: A Tall Tale about a Giant Woman with a Great Big Heart.*
Illustrated by Raúl Colón. New York: Alfred A. Knopf, 2005.

From a clever, inventive tall tale, Pat Mora has created a vibrant rendition of
the beautiful Doña Flor, a gentle and loving Mother Earth figure whose generosity of spirit is equal only to her size. In this delightful story set in the
canyons and valleys of the Spanish-speaking Southwest, Doña Flor has grown
into a giant lady, a caring woman who gets to the root of the problem that
affects the peace and security of her loved ones. From the opening pages, the
reader can see that Doña Flor is filled with serenity. Though some children call

her "Big Foot" and others whisper about her, Doña Flor is special in their eyes. She always makes stacks of tortillas big enough for everyone to share. She delights in reading stories and poems to the children and animals around her. Doña Flor is indeed a giant lady with a great big heart.

From *Doña Flor: A Tall Tale about a Giant Woman with a Great Big Heart*, by Pat Mora

Doña Flor had work to do. But first she looked around the village. Where were her neighbors? Then she heard, "*Rrrr-oarrr! Rrrr-oarrr!*"

Ryan, Pam Muñoz. *Becoming Naomi León.* New York: Scholastic, 2004.
Naomi Soledad León Outlaw suddenly finds that the most troubling thing about her life is not the boys who make fun of her name. When her mother reappears in her life, she intrudes on the cozy world that Naomi has lived in with Gram and her brother, Owen. Her mother cannot accept Owen's disability nor Naomi's soft voice and reticent personality, but she nevertheless proclaims that she wants Naomi to come to live with her and her new boyfriend. Naomi realizes that she has found security and love with Gram and Owen, and she fears that this move will disrupt her life once again. The next thing she knows, Gram is taking desperate measures to find their father and a solution to their dilemma. Their travels take them to Oaxaca in time for the holiday festivities and the famous *La Noche de los Rábanos* festival. Naomi's carving talent not only helps her stay calm but also brings her the thing she wants most—an opportunity to be with her father.

From *Becoming Naomi León*, by Pam Muñoz Ryan

[Owen] shook his head. "I think she never wanted me when I was a baby because I wasn't . . . you know, like everyone else, and I think she doesn't want me now."

"But Gram wanted us, Owen. And our father. Those are the good things. We were lucky for that." I scooted over close to him and put my arm around his shoulders while we waited.

2004
MEDAL WINNER

Alvarez, Julia. *Before We Were Free*. New York: Alfred A. Knopf, 2002.

Cotorrita, or Little Parrot, is a nickname Papi gave to Anita because she talks too much and sometimes asks too many questions. But her questions are understandable because many things are changing, and they are changing much too fast for twelve-year-old Anita. Life in the Dominican Republic has become uncertain and dangerous, and with the help of the American Consul, Anita's extended family is quietly and quickly being swept out of the country and into the United States. General Trujillo, "*El Jefe*," is a dictator to be feared, and when his soldiers arrive at Anita's house, she gets her first glimpse of the SIM, the *policia secreta* who investigate everyone and are responsible for making them disappear. Anita wonders, Where is Tío Toni, and did the SIM make him disappear?

Before We Were Free is the engaging story of one girl's coming-of-age set against a backdrop of fear and secrets. Powerful, and at times intense, this book takes readers on a journey of fear and anguish that will cause them to pray for the rescue of Anita and her family.

From *Before We Were Free*, by Julia Alvarez

Lying in the dark, I start seeing visions of El Jefe lying in a puddle of disgusting blood, and Papi and Tío Toni standing beside the body, and I feel sick to my stomach. Then I hear a sob.

HONOR

Osa, Nancy. *Cuba 15*. New York: Delacorte Press, 2003.

Violet Paz is about to get more than she bargained for. At age fifteen, you'd think she would be old enough to make her own decisions about whether or not to have a birthday party. Right? Wrong! Her Cuban grandmother insists that Violet have a *quinceañera*, the traditional Latina fifteenth birthday celebration, to mark her entry into womanhood. Certain that she'll be allowed to choose her own clothes for the party, Violet agrees. Although she is half Cuban, she has never been to Cuba, and anytime she asks questions about the country, her grandparents become sad and her dad gets angry. She does not feel at all Cuban. After all, with her green eyes and almost-blond hair, who would believe she was Cuban? Between Violet's Polish mother—ever a planner—and her grandmother, the *quinceañera*, or *quince* for short, is a done deal. Planned are the invitations, the band, the fittings, and more. Doesn't her *abuela* remember that Violet never wears dresses?

Cuba 15 humorously and poignantly tells the story of Violet Paz as she prepares unwillingly for her *quinceañera*. Despite her reluctance, she ends up on a journey of self-discovery that leads her to truly value and understand her Cuban heritage for the first time.

From *Cuba 15*, by Nancy Osa

On the way out, I caught sight of myself in the hall mirror. It was like one of those moments when you see your reflection in a store window, and not realizing it's you, say to yourself, She's looking *good*! And then you go, Hey, that's me!

Pérez, Amada Irma. *My Diary from Here to There / Mi diario de aquí hasta allá*. Illustrated by Maya Christina Gonzalez. San Francisco: Children's Book Press, 2002.

When Amada overhears her mamá and papá whisper about moving to the United States, she finds that she cannot sleep, so she pulls out her diary, where she writes down her deepest fears. The idea of moving to a strange place and leaving her beloved Mexico behind is more than she can handle. The next morning, she realizes that her fears have come true, as Mamá explains that the whole family will be moving to Los Angeles, California. How can that be? Her brothers are excited about the move and can hardly wait. Is she the only one scared to leave Juárez, the only home she has ever known? Mamá and Papá keep talking about all the opportunities in the United States. But what will happen if Amada cannot learn English, and worse yet, what if she is not allowed to speak Spanish?

This story is a touching account of a family emigrating from Mexico to California. A bilingual picture book, this young girl's diary chronicles the family's anxiety, excitement, and uncertainty as they leave the only home they have known to start a new life in a new country.

From *My Diary from Here to There / Mi diario de aquí hasta allá*, by Amada Irma Pérez

Finally! Papá sent our green cards—we're going to cross the border at last! He can't come for us but will meet us in Los Angeles.

2002
MEDAL WINNER

Ryan, Pam Muñoz. *Esperanza Rising*. New York: Scholastic, 2000.

Like the mythical phoenix, Esperanza Ortega must rise from the ashes of her former life to begin anew. On the eve of her thirteenth birthday, Esperanza's father is murdered, and her life as the beloved daughter of a rich landowner is changed forever. With the assistance of faithful servants, she and her mother escape the clutches of her greedy uncles and travel to California. There they must work as *campesinos* in the fields to survive. As she changes from a pampered *niña* to a worn-out laborer, Esperanza's view of life changes as well. She gains a greater understanding of others and of the meaning of responsibility and empathy. The chapter headings not only establish setting by naming the seasonal crop but also sometimes foreshadow the mood of the chapter. For example, the first chapter heading is "Las Uvas," or "Grapes," and Ryan describes the dry afternoon when the clusters were heavy and waiting to be picked. Esperanza eventually finds strength in the land and the love that surround her, even though she is living in poverty. Like the rose that was transplanted from her father's garden, Esperanza learns that life can have beauty in the midst of thorns.

From *Esperanza Rising*, by Pam Muñoz Ryan

"No hay rosa sin espinas." There is no rose without thorns. Esperanza smiled, knowing that Abuelita wasn't talking about flowers at all, but that there was no life without difficulties.

HONOR

Alarcón, Francisco X. *Iguanas in the Snow and Other Winter Poems / Iguanas en la nieve y otros poemas de invierno*. Illustrated by Maya Christina Gonzalez. San Francisco: Children's Book Press, 2001.

Francisco Alarcón captures the beauty and joy of winter in this bilingual collection of poems. The reader is introduced to such San Francisco sights as cable cars, the Mission District, colorful murals, and the sea lions at Fisherman's Wharf. The word *iguanas* in the title refers to the green jackets and pants the family purchased at the army surplus store to wear when they play in the mountain snow. The *poemas* are short but have substantial themes that are easily grasped and equally effective in both English and Spanish. Maya Christina Gonzalez's colorful illustrations occasionally become part of the poem, as in "First Snowfall," where a word from the poem is found within a snowflake. Other titles in Alarcón's collection of seasonal poetry books include *Laughing Tomatoes and Other Spring Poems, From the Bellybutton of the Moon and Other*

Summer Poems, and *Angels Ride Bikes and Other Fall Poems*. Alarcón celebrates family and community through these succinct but skillfully crafted verses.

From *Iguanas in the Snow and Other Winter Poems / Iguanas en la nieve y otros poemas de invierno*, by Francisco X. Alarcón

To Write Poetry
  we must
  first touch
  smell and taste
  every word

Jiménez, Francisco. *Breaking Through*. Boston: Houghton Mifflin, 2001.

Francisco Jiménez described the immigration of his family from Mexico to California in *The Circuit*. This sequel continues the story of Jiménez's family into his teen years and through his graduation from high school. The courage and determination of the family to succeed and thrive provide a heartrending backdrop to the struggles they must endure. The story begins with the family's deportation back to Mexico. But because Francisco and his brother Roberto can get papers and jobs, they are sent back to California on their own until the rest of the family can join them. Francisco and Roberto work hard, both in school and at their jobs, but they also try to find time for a little fun. Francisco's first crush and his first brush with prejudice are humiliating, but his self-discipline and resolve help him to make his place in his school and community. But as the boys make their places in the world, their father's physical and emotional pain as he struggles to accept the growth and strength of his oldest sons causes family tensions. Keeping the family together becomes difficult. The story ends with Francisco heading off to college and a new life of hope and success.

From *Breaking Through*, by Francisco Jiménez

Papá asked me why I like school so much. I told him I liked learning and wanted to be a teacher. . . . He said, "Don't be stupid. Only rich people become teachers."

2000
MEDAL WINNER

Ada, Alma Flor. *Under the Royal Palms: A Childhood in Cuba*. New York: Atheneum Books for Young Readers, 1998.

Born in Camagüey, Cuba, Ada remembers the daily routine of living in her family's home, La Quinta Simoni, in this memoir of growing up in a small town. She cherishes the simple rituals of her life—spending time with her grandmother, gathering wild flowers named *maravillas*, and watching bats appear after nightfall. Things were sometimes so routine that any out-of-the-ordinary occurrences, like getting lost while playing in the fields, stuck in her mind and left lasting impressions.

But some of her memories are devastating, such as when her uncle loses his life piloting a plane in bad weather or when her special ballet teacher collapses mid-performance and eventually dies from the cancer that caused the collapse.

At one point Ada's extended family purchases an old jewelry store and moves into a house behind it. Every family member contributes to the business to make it successful, and they eventually spend their nights making affordable Nativity scenes with clay figurines. Many photographs of Ada and her family are included in this book, which is named after the majestic royal palm trees that symbolize an independent Cuba. The title may also describe this family standing tall under all circumstances.

From *Under the Royal Palms: A Childhood in Cuba,* by Alma Flor Ada

Life in a small town had a very special flavor. . . . Any experience outside the ordinary received an enormous amount of attention and became the focus of everyone's conversation for many days to come.

HONOR

Alarcón, Francisco X. *From the Bellybutton of the Moon and Other Summer Poems / Del ombligo de la luna y otros poemas de verano*. Illustrated by Maya Christina Gonzalez. San Francisco: Children's Book Press, 1998.

This summer edition of Alarcón's bilingual poetry series focuses on his childhood summers in Mexico. Every summer, Alarcón and his family drove across Mexico's western mountain range to his grandmother's town of Atoyac in Jalisco. There he enjoyed Auntie Reginalda's breakfasts, saw Uncle Vicente sit in his rocker after farming all day, learned his first Spanish letters from Grandpa Pancho, and counted on daily five o'clock rain showers.

Many of the poems are universal in describing summertime: the weather is hot and sunny, the grass is green, the trees and flowers are in bloom, and the ocean is alive. Other poems are universal to childhood: almost all the poems embody play. In "Mariposa," Alarcón's favorite cow is so named "because she has the mark of a butterfly on her face," and he imagines "she really is a butterfly." Accompanied by Maya Christina Gonzalez's magnificent, vibrant illustrations, poems such as "Island," "Sea," and "Question" invite you to jump into the ocean and have fun with Alarcón and his siblings. In "Ode to My Shoes," Alarcón reminisces about shoes that, during the night, "stretch and loosen their laces" to "wake up cheerful relaxed so soft" the next morning.

Ultimately, it is Alarcón's sense of humor that brings the poems to life and makes them appealing. There is even a poem about the family's bilingual dog who barks "*guau guau*" in Spanish and then repeats "bowwow" in English.

From the title poem of *From the Bellybutton of the Moon and Other Summer Poems / Del ombligo de la luna y otros poemas de verano*, by Francisco X. Alarcón

"Mexico" says my grandma

"means: from the bellybutton of the moon"

"don't forget your origin my son"

maybe that's why

whenever I now say "Mexico"

I feel like touching my bellybutton.

Herrera, Juan Felipe. *Laughing Out Loud, I Fly: Poems in English and Spanish*. Drawings by Karen Barbour. New York: Joanna Cotler Books, 1998.

Influenced by Pablo Picasso's *Hunk of Skin*, Herrera wanted to write about his childhood. The twenty-one poems, each in both English and Spanish, play on words. Like Picasso, Herrera wanted to paint words that celebrate a different way of seeing the world. He wanted to explore the themes of play, laughing out loud, and flying. This progression starts off with play. He plays as he writes the poems, creating unusual pairings. All his playing makes readers laugh out loud. And once they are laughing out loud, they start to fly!

Each poem is somehow tied together by its title. Herrera remembers something from his childhood, then continues to describe the memory in each poem. Events, objects, family members, and food all make appearances in his poetry. Occasional Spanish words are included in the English versions of the poems. It is almost as if Herrera has returned to his childhood, recaptured the nonsense-type language children eventually grow out of, and is enjoying playing within his poems, which, of course, make him laugh out loud and fly.

From the title poem of *Laughing Out Loud, I Fly: Poems in English and Spanish*, by Juan Felipe Herrera

Laughing out loud, I fly, toward the good things,
To catch Mamá Lucha on the sidewalk, after
school, waiting for the green-striped bus,
on the side of the neighborhood store, next to almonds,
José's tiny wooden mule, the wiseboy from San Diego,
teeth split apart, like mine in the coppery afternoon

1998
MEDAL WINNER

Martinez, Victor. *Parrot in the Oven: Mi vida*. New York: Joanna Cotler Books, 1996.

Fourteen-year-old Manny Hernandez lives with his family in a government housing project in Fresno, California, where so-called normal life is challenged daily by one traumatic event after another. His is a culture where alcoholism, guns, gangs, and racism are an ordinary part of everyday life. His father is an irregularly employed alcoholic who manages to get himself arrested at home in his family's presence for stubbornly refusing to let go of a weapon that has sentimental value for him. Manny also witnesses his older sister Magda's miscarriage and subsequent pain as he accompanies his mother and sister to the hospital, traveling by public transportation because they have no car. Manny's mother might have asked one of the neighbors for a ride, but she refuses to give them their daily dose of gossip at Magda's expense.

Manny is keenly aware of his family's socioeconomic reality, contrary to his father's perception that Manny is too young and naive to understand all that is going on. The metaphoric title is borrowed from a Mexican saying that likens a parrot to one who does not quite realize that he or she is in the thick of a situation until it is too late.

Like a true Aztec storyteller, Martinez is flawless in his ability to provide a well-told story that is rich in metaphor and imbued with language that helps to transform an ordinary coming-of-age story into a truly remarkable work of literary art.

From *Parrot in the Oven: Mi vida*, by Victor Martinez

In that instant of trying to call out to Eddie, everything changed. It was like I'd finally seen my own face and recognized myself; recognized who I really should be.

HONOR

Alarcón, Francisco X. *Laughing Tomatoes and Other Spring Poems / Jitomates risueños y otros poemas de primavera*. Illustrated by Maya Christina Gonzalez. San Francisco: Children's Book Press, 1997.

Laughing Tomatoes—the title itself is a delight, and Francisco Alarcón's twenty poems are silly and thought-provoking. He strikes a balance with the selected poems—a balance that reflects the varying and realistic moments in life. Sometimes it is appropriate to play, other times to rest and sleep, and still others to stop and honor a holiday (such as Cinco de Mayo) or a hero (such as César Chávez). Alarcón's poems offer moments of pause for appreciation of everyday things: the beat of the washing machine, an ode to corn, the tortilla as "a tasty round of applause for the sun," or "the sweet tender hearts" that are strawberries. Because the poems are bilingual, the pages become full with real life in a multicultural world. Gonzalez's illustrations capture the cadence of each passage in English and Spanish.

Whether reading the English, the Spanish, or both, readers are kept in a playful frame of mind by Maya Christina Gonzalez's illustrations. Readers will want to hang upside down from trees, dance on the kitchen floor, let their braids fly while doing somersaults, and keep the pets close by. This is family. This is fun. Gonzalez interprets Alarcón's poetry with full-lipped smiles on suns and mountains, bouncing fruits and vegetables, graceful birds, scenes of dreamy sleep, and the visage of César Chávez above an oak tree planted in his honor. Her colors are vivid. The faces of the children, Abuelita, and the pets express awe, joy, and reflection. The textures and colors of the children's hair and complexions are diverse, as they should be, quite naturally, in any Latino family or community. This is a joyful poetry book to be used in many ways, such as learning verse or recalling vivid memories of childhood.

From *Laughing Tomatoes and Other Spring Poems / Jitomates risueños y otros poemas de primavera*, by Francisco X. Alarcón

Each tortilla
is a tasty
round of applause
for the sun
Cada tortilla
es una sabrosa
ronda de aplausos
para el sol

—from "Tortilla" / "*La Tortilla*"

Martinez, Floyd. *Spirits of the High Mesa*. Houston: Arte Público Press, 1997.

Flavio has a close relationship with the patriarch of Capulin, a small village in northern New Mexico. *El Grande* is his grandfather, and from him Flavio learns, sometimes painfully, to hunt, chop wood, raise sheep for food, and live with nature in a respectful way. His grandfather's indigenous roots underscore hunting practices and seasonal chores. There should be no needless death, no waste, but respect for all wildlife. Water must be rerouted from the creek to make the *acequia* in the winter, and the cattle and horses must be branded in the summer. All the villagers come together to work in the community for the good of the whole village.

This peaceful but hardworking life comes to an end with progress: first electricity, then the U.S. Forest Service, then the *molino*—the sawmill. Progress is seductive and in some ways practical, but it is certainly not understanding of traditions. New immigrants have come to work in the sawmill, people from Oklahoma and Arkansas. With the newcomers, tension rises as customs differ and misunderstandings occur. There are fights, a murder, and children's names even become anglicized.

All are affected by change, especially *El Grande* and Flavio, because their bond is at stake. Despite this circumstance, there is still work to do, fights to get into, baseball to be played, pathways to explore, and more questions to be asked of *El Grande*, because he has special knowledge.

Floyd Martinez offers us a glimpse into a historically unique Hispanic experience. *Spirits of the High Mesa* will be enjoyed by readers who like historical fiction, stories of country life, or stories of special friendships.

From *Spirits of the High Mesa*, by Floyd Martinez

I came home to the cabin with trouble on my mind. I wanted to ride with El Grande to the *cerro*, but what about the game? I would miss the game. But then, I would hurt his feelings. What would I do?

1996
MEDAL WINNER

Ortiz Cofer, Judith. *An Island Like You: Stories of the Barrio*. New York: Orchard Books, 1995.

In one story, Rita is a blossoming, sassy young teen who lives with her parents in the tenement building known as "El Building" in Paterson, New Jersey. She and her girlfriend, Meli, each tell their parents that they will spend the night at the other's house, but the plot is foiled when Meli's little sister tells her parents that the girls have gone to Joey Molieri's house. Rita is placed under house arrest before being shipped off to Puerto Rico to live with her grandparents as punishment. Expecting to serve out her summer in utter boredom, she learns to appreciate her grandparents and their way of life, replete with household roosters and the weird motions of spiritual healings for *mala influencia*.

In a second story, the elderly residents of the tenement building mistake Arturo for a punk because he spikes his purple hair. When his parents reprimand him, he grows furious and decides to leave home. In haste, he pulls out his meager savings, mistakenly throwing "Willy" Shakespeare into the dumpster. While seeking solace at St. Joseph's Church, his conversation with the old church keeper, Johann, reignites his love for poetry and literature. He returns to the dumpster to learn what poem his friend Kenny will be reciting in the next day's class.

These and other carefully crafted, interconnected stories provide vivid and sometimes subtle portraits of young Puerto Rican teenagers who are connected to each other, living as neighbors, classmates, and residents in the same tenement unit known as "El Building." The stories serve as a landscape for the lives of impressionable teens as they wrestle with a variety of cultural and social issues in the search for their own identities.

From *An Island Like You: Stories of the Barrio*, by Judith Ortiz Cofer

See, for the guys of the barrio, reading poetry is like an unnatural act. *Liking* poetry makes you suspicious as to your sexual preference. Unless you're a girl. It's so stupid I can't even explain it to myself. It's just words. Poetry is like the words of a song, and these guys would kill to write songs and be rock stars.

—from "Arturo's Flight"

HONOR

González, Lucía M., reteller. *The Bossy Gallito / El gallo de bodas: A Traditional Cuban Folktale*. Illustrated by Lulu Delacre. New York: Scholastic, 1994.

Tío Perico, a parrot, is getting married and has invited his family and friends, including his nephew, a rooster, to the wedding. The little rooster, one of the bossiest roosters a person could ever encounter, dresses in his finest clothes for the wedding. On the way to the wedding, however, he faces a major dilemma: he detects two kernels of corn on the side of the road and must decide whether he should eat the kernels and risk getting his beak dirty. Temptation gets the better of him, setting in motion his series of panicked cries for help. This delightfully told cumulative Cuban folktale is set in Little Havana, Miami's foremost Cuban neighborhood, known as *la Calle Ocho* (Eighth Avenue). The illustrations accentuate the lush flora and fauna that are typical of the Florida region of the Hispanic Caribbean. In keeping with the wedding theme, Delacre skillfully uses watercolors, colored pencils, and gouache to frame the text and illustrations into oval-shaped portraits. Included are a Spanish glossary to encourage readers to practice the Spanish words and author's and illustrator's notes that add further context to the story and the illustrations.

From *The Bossy Gallito / El gallo de bodas: A Traditional Cuban Folktale*, retold by Lucía M. González

The little Gallito thanked his good friend *el sol* with a long:

¡QUI-QUI-RI-QUI!
COCK-A-DOODLE-DOO!

Soto, Gary. *Baseball in April and Other Stories*. New York: Harcourt, 1990.

These eleven stories feature adolescent Latino protagonists, both male and female, who find themselves in situations that require them to come up with their own solutions to their problems. In "Mother and Daughter," Yolie is Mrs. Moreno's only daughter. Unemployed, they live on meager subsidies and are too poor to buy much of anything new, much less a new dress for Yolie's upcoming dance. Trying to both make ends meet and satisfy her daughter's needs and wants, Mrs. Moreno buys black dye with which to convert Yolie's old, white summer dress into a smashing new dress. But what she didn't count on was the rain, which creates a most embarrassing moment for Yolie as she stands helplessly and watches the dye on her dress drip into a puddle in the middle of the bathroom floor.

In "Seventh Grade," Victor discovers on his first day of school that Teresa, a girl he has long admired, is in the same French class that he is. Caught in the act of clowning and yet wanting to make a good first impression, he pretends to have a sophisticated conversation in French with his teacher, who is quick to recognize the dynamics of the situation and cuts him some slack.

Together, these stories offer readers a glimpse into the idiosyncrasies of everyday Latino teen life. They reflect the everyday situations of young kids caught in that in-between stage called adolescence and show how they manage to maneuver through it unscathed. *Baseball in April and Other Stories* exemplifies an old Mexican proverb: "*Cada cabeza es un mundo*" (each head is its own world).

Illustrations

Plate 1. From *Doña Flor*, by Pat Mora. Illustrated by Raúl Colón

Plate 2. From *Chato's Kitchen*, by Gary Soto. Illustrated by Susan Guevara

Chato and Novio Boy were in the living room grooming themselves for the party. After five hours of cooking they were so hungry that each time a bird swooped past the window, their gray eyes grew narrow and their mouths watered.

When they heard a rap on the door they grinned at each other. It was like a delivery service with mice instead of pizza!

"We brought Chorizo," Mami mouse called.

Sausage! Chato and Novio Boy danced, and with clean paws they gave each other a "low four."

"We can have *chorizo con* mice." Novio Boy grinned.

Plate 3. From *Snapshots from the Wedding*, by Gary Soto. Illustrated by Stephanie Garcia

Plate 4. From *Magic Windows: Cut-Paper Art and Stories*, by Carmen Lomas Garza

"Just a minute, Señor Calavera,"
Grandma Beetle said. "I will go with
you right away, I have just **THREE**
pounds of corn to make into tortillas."

Señor Calavera rolled his eyes.
He had to be very patient sometimes.

TRES Three stacks of tortillas,
counted Señor Calavera, and he put
on his hat.

Plate 5. From *Just a Minute: A Trickster Tale and Counting Book*, by Yuyi Morales

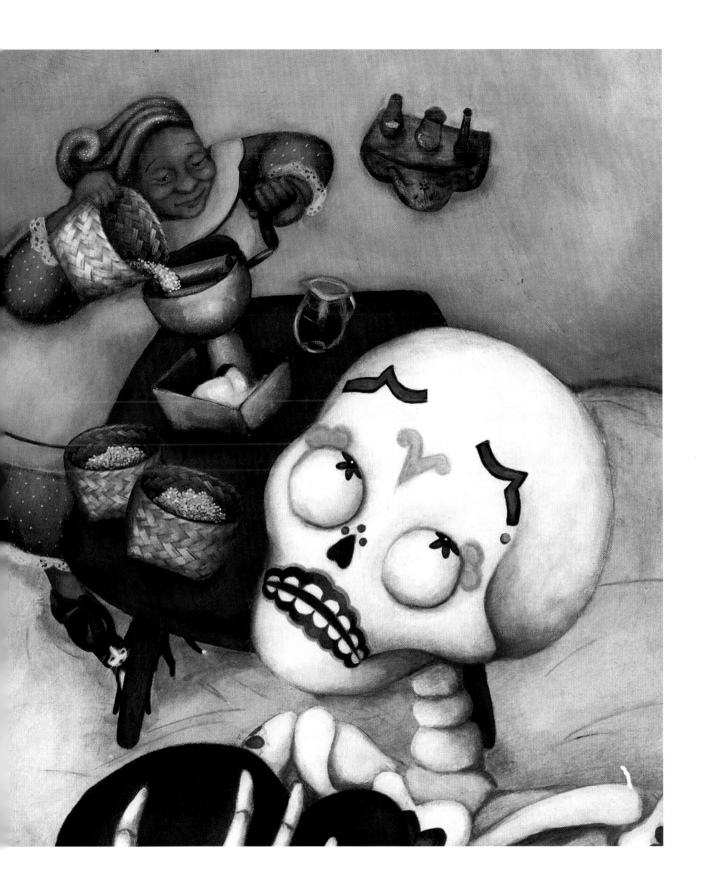

The *pachanga* lasted until the sun went down, the moon came up, and the neighbors started throwing shoes at them to stop the racket. Novio Boy stayed overnight, sleeping on a new cat cushion, his present from Chato, the coolest *carnal* in all of *el barrio*.

Plate 6. From *Chato and the Party Animals*, by Gary Soto. Illustrated by Susan Guevara

From *Baseball in April and Other Stories*, by Gary Soto

It was his hope that after he retired, he and his wife would return to Mexico, to Jalapa, where all the people would look on them with respect. Not one day would pass without the butcher or barber or pharmacist or ambitious children with dollar signs in their eyes waving to "*El Millionario*."

—from "Two Dreamers"

Illustrator Awards

Mora, Pat. *Doña Flor: A Tall Tale about a Giant Woman with a Great Big Heart*. Illustrated by **Raúl Colón**. New York: Alfred A. Knopf, 2005.

For Mora's delightful story of Doña Flor, a gentle and loving Mother Earth figure whose generosity of spirit is equal only to her size, Raúl Colón has crafted giant-size figures of Doña Flor using a combination of watercolor washes, etching, and colored and litho pencils. With effective use of broad strokes, scratchboard, and swirls, he transports young readers directly into Doña Flor's imaginary village. There, Huck Finn–like children explore the river's bends as they float along in their rafts made from leftover tortillas. Colón's artwork offers a wholesome exercise in perspective. Children will ponder concepts of big and little when giant Doña Flor is contrasted with a puny puma, or as other animals and people are portrayed as miniature figures. Colón's artwork is sure to delight little ones intrigued with concepts of size.

HONOR

Delacre, Lulu. *Arrorró, Mi Niño: Latino Lullabies and Gentle Games*. New York: Lee and Low, 2004.

"Sweet lullabies and gentle games" is how Delacre describes this lovely bilingual collection of fifteen lullabies and rhymes—early childhood lore gathered from Latinas of all ages and all walks of life. Delacre depicts the vibrancy of life in the United States as Latina mothers go about their daily chores of living and caring for their young ones in the United States. She paints Latina moms (and a grandmother) as active, engaging agents, singing, talking, or cooing to their little ones in a variety of settings, including a farmhouse, a schoolhouse hall, a library lapsit, a park, a Salvadoran restaurant, and a modern art gallery. Rendered in oil washes, Delacre's colorful, warm illustrations tenderly capture those joyful moments of mother-child interactions in full-page and double-page pictures that alternate with the verse. The accompanying musical arrangements and Spanish lyrics include English translations of the verses.

Bernier-Grand, Carmen T. *César: ¡Sí, Se Puede! Yes, We Can!* Illustrated by
    David Diaz. New York: Marshall Cavendish, 2004.

Using computer technology and luminous colors, David Diaz evokes the spirit of both César Chávez and his cause. The stylized figures are reminiscent of Mexican folk art, and the soft palette is influenced by the sunlight, brown earth, green crops, and blue sky that are prevalent in the lives of *campesinos*. Infusions of soft purple and bright red add dramatic touches to the depictions of events in Chávez's life. By keeping the illustrations light, Diaz balances the seriousness of the poems they illustrate. The effect for the reader is a sense that there is both beauty and hardship in the lives of Chávez, his family, and his fellow organizers.

Brown, Monica. *My Name Is Celia: The Life of Celia Cruz / Me llamo Celia:*
    La vida de Celia Cruz. Illustrated by **Rafael López**. Flagstaff, AZ: Luna
    Rising, 2004.

Celia Cruz, known simply as Celia, was the queen of salsa—a blend of Latin music and jazz. Monica Brown brings Celia to life by having her tell the story of her childhood love of music, her family, and her homeland. Celia instructs us to "close our eyes and listen" to the musical words: "Bum, bum bum!" and "like the waves of the ocean hitting the roof of my mouth, . . . the streets of Havana, . . . my mother's kitchen, . . . a tummy full of beans and bananas and rice, . . . a cup of warm coffee with sugar." Then "Abre los ojos / Open your eyes" to see Rafael López's depiction of Celia with dancing earrings, beautiful bracelets, sparkling brown eyes, and swirling, curling hair dancing and singing amid butterflies, musical notes, stars, and hearts. López's illustrations embody the sensations associated with listening to salsa: liveliness, joy, energy, and a desire to move and to dance. Although Celia's impact on Latino culture and music in the United States is emphasized, this picture book biography also offers the story of Celia's childhood, her heartache at leaving Cuba, and her experiences of racism. López magically captures the essence of Celia's story— that music is rejuvenating and joyful and brings people together.

2004
MEDAL WINNER

Morales, Yuyi. *Just a Minute: A Trickster Tale and Counting Book*. San
    Francisco: Chronicle Books, 2003.

When Grandma Beetle opens her door, Señor Calavera is there waiting to take her on her journey—her time has come. "Just a minute, Señor Calavera,"

Grandma Beetle responds. She is certainly not ready and so begins a series of activities to annoy, frustrate, and confuse Señor Calavera.

Yuyi Morales's energetic and playful illustrations capture the essence of Mexican culture with bold and humorous motifs. Señor Calavera looks like a sugar skull, and his expressions are constantly changing. Grandma Beetle's home is also brilliantly illustrated. From the clay pots on the stove to the red chiles strung from the ceiling to melting cheeses and piñatas being filled with candy, readers will appreciate the festivity found throughout the pages. The story is not bilingual; however, the book is also a counting book and allows readers to count in both English and Spanish. Count to *diez* and count to ten in this tale of one character about to be tricked by the other. Can you guess who gets tricked?

HONOR

Andrews-Goebel, Nancy. *The Pot That Juan Built*. Illustrated by **David Diaz**. New York: Lee and Low Books, 2002.

Juan Quezada is a renowned potter from Mata Ortiz, Mexico, who rediscovered the primitive process that the Casas Grandes people used to make pots. This cumulative rhyme tells his story. David Diaz's computer-generated illustrations at times glow, giving the reader the sensation of sun beating down on the hot desert. His artwork accompanies two stories told at the same time. On the left side of the book is the familiar rhyme that begins "This is the pot that Juan built," which is reminiscent of the rhyme in "The House That Jack Built." On the book's right-hand side, the biography of Juan Quezada unfolds, and the reader learns when he was born, when he became a potter, and what process he uses to make his pottery. We learn that the flames must be sizzling hot in order for a pot to be fired and that his paintbrushes are made from human hair. We also discover that in order for the pot to shine, it must be rubbed by a tool made of bone. Diaz excels at illuminating each page in this easy-to-read biography, which includes additional information about pottery, Mata Ortiz, and Juan Quezada in an afterword.

Krull, Kathleen. *Harvesting Hope: The Story of César Chávez*. Illustrated by **Yuyi Morales**. New York: Harcourt, 2003.

La Causa (the Cause) and César Chávez go hand in hand. Chávez is the civil rights leader who worked tirelessly to procure better wages and better working conditions for migrant farm workers in the United States. Yuyi Morales brings his cause to life through illustrations in this touching biography by Kathleen Krull. In the opening pages, the reader sees a magical story unfold as children gather under netting to listen to stories about Mexico while another child listens in the background as she enjoys her watermelon. On another two-page spread, disappointment and heartache are apparent on the faces of Mama and her kids when they realize that they have lost their ranch and will have to move.

In Morales's depiction of the backbreaking labor of thinning lettuce all day, one can almost feel the workers' hot muscle spasms. Readers will also feel embarrassed by the intolerance of some when they encounter the illustration of Chávez with eyes closed and around his neck a sign that reads "I am a clown. I speak Spanish." In the end, readers will cheer the cause that Chávez worked so hard for and will understand the life of a man who sought to make things better for others by founding the National Farm Workers Association and by leading the longest protest march in U.S. history to bring awareness to the plight of migrant workers.

Pérez, L. King. *First Day in Grapes*. Illustrated by **Robert Casilla**. New York: Lee and Low Books, 2002.

Chico has had many first days, and it is while in third grade that he has his first day in grapes. Chico is the son of migrant workers, and his family travels from one migrant camp to another, to wherever crops need to be picked. Casilla vividly and realistically portrays Chico and his family throughout the pages of the book. Readers can share Chico's unhappiness when he does not want to go to school because the kids call him names, his pride when his teacher discovers his ease with math and enrolls him in the math fair, and his fear when he needs to stand up for himself against the class bullies. Casilla does a good job of capturing Chico's emotions, and readers will enjoy knowing Chico and cheering for his success.

2002
MEDAL WINNER

Soto, Gary. *Chato and the Party Animals*. Illustrated by **Susan Guevara**. New York: G. P. Putnam's Sons, 2000.

No one loves a fiesta more than Chato, the coolest low-riding cat in the barrio. Chato notices his *carnal*, his best friend, Novio Boy, wearing a sad face at Chorizo's birthday party. He learns that not only has Novio Boy never had a birthday party, but because he was born in the pound, he doesn't even remember his *mami*. Chato decides to hold a birthday party for his best *amigo*. He orders a cake with mouse-colored frosting, makes a fish-shaped piñata, and decorates the yard. He invites everyone in the neighborhood, from Chorizo the dog to the mouse family. But he forgets to invite the guest of honor! The *pachanga* is set to begin, but Novio Boy is nowhere to be seen. After searching the neighborhood in vain, the party turns into a wake, with Novio Boy's friends certain that he is lost, kidnapped, or even *muerto* (dead). But Novio Boy returns, and the joyous reunion with his friends sets off the best fiesta ever, lasting long into the night.

Susan Guevara brings Chato and his barrio neighborhood to life with acrylics that add spirit and movement to the story. The neighborhood, modeled after barrios in Los Angeles, is full of murals, color, and the ambiance of a close-knit community. The added touches of Novio Boy's guardian angel *mami* and symbols from Chicano culture add a sense of magical realism to this engaging tale of *familia*, friendship, and *comunidad*.

HONOR

Montes, Marisa, reteller. *Juan Bobo Goes to Work: A Puerto Rican Folktale*.
Illustrated by **Joe Cepeda**. New York: HarperCollins, 2000.

Poor, silly Juan Bobo. He gets everything confused. Taken from a Puerto Rican folktale, this story follows the adventures of "simple John" as he goes to work for a neighboring farmer. His poor *mamá* tries to teach him how to bring home his pay each day, but he never seems to get it right. This tale is familiar to children from many cultures, but it never fails to elicit giggles. The tale ends satisfactorily with the merry laugh from a *señorita*, and all is right with Juan Bobo and his *mamá*.

Joe Cepeda's brilliant oil palette brings life and luminosity to Juan Bobo's story. Portrayed as a simple, smiling *muchacho*, Juan Bobo, and his world, are depicted in the vibrant colors of the Puerto Rican countryside.

2000
MEDAL WINNER

Lomas Garza, Carmen. *Magic Windows: Cut-Paper Art and Stories / Ventanas mágicas: Papel picado y relatos*. Translated by Francisco X. Alarcón. San Francisco: Children's Book Press, 1999.

Lomas Garza used a craft-knife technique to make the intricate tissue-paper cutout designs in this collection of cut-paper art and stories. Many of the depictions are of Lomas Garza's family, childhood, and Mexican heritage. The challenge was to make all the pieces of paper in these "magic windows" connect.

Some of the items depicted are animals of significance to Mexican culture, such as horned toads (now endangered), hummingbirds, and all the animals in the waters surrounding the Aztec capital city, Tenochititlán. Other magic windows depict Mexican symbols. "Eagle with Rattlesnake" includes the two animals on the Mexican flag's emblem in a particularly complex paper cutout. Two skeletons dance together on the Day of the Dead, the Mexican holiday when the dead come back to visit the living. The skirt of a traditional Mexican *jarabe tapatío* dancer is held together by a grid, and interestingly, Lomas Garza has depicted her own hands painting the dancer's skirt.

Many of Lomas Garza's illustrations focus on the work her family does with their hands. Her grandfather's hands cut a *nopal* cactus and water his garden. Her mother's hands roll tortillas and make paper flowers with the rest of the family. Lomas Garza learns these skills from her family and appreciates the time spent doing these activities with them. The final entry, depicting Lomas Garza with her niece and nephews making *papel picado*, reflects the continuation of the family tradition.

HONOR

Ancona, George. *Barrio: José's Neighborhood*. San Diego: Harcourt Brace, 1998.

José lives in San Francisco's diverse Mission District. José attends Spanish-English bilingual class at his school, which also offers a Chinese bilingual class and a black history program. The reader learns about Latino customs, traditions, and history through this photo-essay that follows José through the different aspects of his life and daily routine.

José enjoys going to César Chávez Elementary School and playing with his friends during recess. Someone is painting a large mural of César Chávez on the back of the school, and many murals throughout the barrio tell the story of those who live there. Soccer is very popular, and José has won many trophies during the five years he has played with the neighborhood team. Almost everyone in José's family lives nearby, and food imported from Latin America is readily available in the barrio.

The community comes together to work and celebrate. Children from the different schools rehearse for weeks for the *Carnaval* celebration and parade. People from all cultures march, dance, and share food. They unite to work on the three community gardens. José's school celebrates Halloween in the school yard. Skull masks, sugar skulls, and toys are made for the school-yard celebration as well as altars for businesses, schools, and homes in honor of the Day of the Dead, which is also marked by a nighttime procession. José's birthday is also a great time for a party, complete with friends, family, a piñata, and cake—something universal to all children. All of these events are captured in color photographs by Ancona, with close-ups giving a community feel to José's neighborhood.

Carling, Amelia Lau. *Mama and Papa Have a Store*. New York: Dial Books for Young Readers, 1998.

In this book, the fusion of Spanish, Chinese, and Mayan languages and cultures are seen through the eyes of a young Chinese girl who is not old enough to go to school. After her siblings leave for school each day, she starts her day in her parents' Chinese store in Guatemala City. Various Latino characters sell their wares on the street. Having traveled from far away, a Mayan family, speaking imperfect Spanish, buys thread for their traditional clothing. The young Chinese girl's mother buys fresh tofu from a Chinese seller. In Chinese, they talk about their hometown in China, which they left because of war. We follow the young girl through the events of the rest of the day, which include a black-out because of rain, until it is time to close the store.

Rich in cultural lessons, this book embraces Guatemala's three cultures, increasing awareness of customs and traditions with both words and beautiful illustrations. Using watercolor and gouache, Carling brings her illustrations to life with bright colors and extraordinary detail—the Mayan clothes, the Latino artist's paintings, the lunch table complete with chopsticks for each family member. Scenes that give the reader a larger overall view—such as the patio of the family home, the roof on which the children glide, and the Chinese store—do so without losing any of the minutia of daily life. The young girl tells us that the store has everything in it, and the illustrations certainly prove it.

Slate, Joseph. *The Secret Stars*. Illustrated by **Felipe Dávalos**. New York: Marshall Cavendish, 1998.

Set in New Mexico, this book tells the story of Sila and Pepe, who sleep under a quilt with their grandmother anticipating the arrival of the Three Kings the next morning. Awakened by rain, they worry that the Three Kings will not be able to find them, for there are no visible stars in this weather. The grandmother insists that they sleep, and their grandmother's quilt becomes her wings. As she flies with each grandchild floating beneath her, she points out the secret stars that will guide the Three Kings: the frosted flowers, the spider's web laced with ice, and the rooster's feathers and the deer horns glittering with frost. They hurry home, and the first thing the children notice when they wake the next morning is that their grandmother's veins crisscross like stars. Remembering that it is Three Kings Day, they run out to the barn and find the gifts the Three Kings have left them. They once again see the secret stars as they look at the pines that "have become the Three Kings" and "their crowns and capes . . . are filled with stars."

Dávalos uses acrylic to illustrate this magical story. The grandmother's quilt, the deserted countryside, and the Three Kings themselves are portrayed in the style of the Southwestern United States. The artist also meets the challenge of painting nature's various secret stars.

1998
MEDAL WINNER

Soto, Gary. *Snapshots from the Wedding*. Illustrated by **Stephanie Garcia**. New York: G. P. Putnam's Sons, 1997.

Stephanie Garcia captures the flavor, formality, and fun of a festive wedding through the eyes of Maya, the flower girl. Dressed in pink silk and white anklets with flowers in her hair, Maya, camera in hand, documents the wedding day. The snapshots are Garcia's skillful creation of shadow boxes filled with expressive sculpty-clay figures. Cousin Virginia, the basketball player, jumps high to catch the wedding bouquet. Always the helpful *tío*, Trino jump-starts a family car. Rafael, the handsome groom, appears with his arm in a sling and cast from a softball accident. Tía Marta weeps big tears of joy while Tío Juan itches from his new suit. The juxtaposition of lace, roses, and ribbons with painted smudges of *pollo con mole* on Maya's dress and olives on her clay fingertips bring texture to the fabric of this community celebration.

As for the text, Gary Soto's poetic narrative is in Maya's voice. Clearly, both author and illustrator magically aligned themselves to honor the child's voice and the child's view. Children and adults will enjoy poring over the illustrations.

HONOR

Lomas Garza, Carmen. *In My Family / En mi familia*. San Francisco: Children's Book Press, 1996.

From the embroidered aprons of her mother's dress to the mama cat nursing her three kittens on the cool hardwood floor to the carefully shaped dough of the mouthwatering *empanadas*, Carmen Lomas Garza transports us to her childhood in South Texas with the exquisite detail and vibrant color of her paintings. Plants, animals, food, relatives, neighbors, and friends make up the daily routine and special rituals of an extended Mexican American family. Each painting is a story, a window, a memory, a tradition—a slice of universal life that is also narrated by Lomas Garza. And just when the reader thinks that all details in a scene have been observed, there is yet one more to discover. There is Abuelita in the bottom left-hand corner holding the baby during the dance, and there is the long-tailed lizard crawling up the upper right-hand corner of the window screen while Grandfather cleans the *nopalitos*. And there is the baseball glove and bat put aside on the floor while the grandchildren listen to Grandmother tell the story of *La Llorona*. Lomas Garza, with her voice and her paintbrush, evokes an appreciation of the universal urge to gather together and at the same time educates readers about distinctive Mexican American traditions.

Ada, Alma Flor. *Gathering the Sun: An Alphabet in Spanish and English*.
    Illustrated by **Simón Silva**. English translation by Rosa Zubizarreta.
    New York: Lothrop, Lee, and Shepard, 1997.

Gathering the Sun: An Alphabet in Spanish and English is a bilingual alphabet and poetry book illuminated by sunlight. Simón Silva's gouache illustrations are rich with gold, orange, green, copper, red, and yellow hues. Even the blues and purples seem to have been kissed by sunlight. With these vivid colors Silva visually translates Alma Flor Ada's poems: *T* for *tomates* (tomatoes), *G* for *gracias* (thank you), and *D* for *duraznos* (peaches).

The reflection and transmission of sun take center stage as the illustrations convey the largeness of the fields, the rows, the times of day, the family support, the dreams of children, and, most important, the connectedness of nature, hard work, and the food we eat. The Mexican family in the story shows how hard they work as well as how much they value and respect children. An alphabet book, a book about agriculture and work, a poetry book, a bilingual book, a book of colors, a book that offers insight into an individual family—*Gathering the Sun* has many uses.

Jaffe, Nina. *The Golden Flower: A Taino Myth from Puerto Rico*. Illustrated by
    Enrique O. Sánchez. New York: Simon and Schuster Books for Young
    Readers, 1996.

Dreamy, transparent, colorful illustrations by Enrique Sánchez transport us through the Taino myth of how the island of Boriquén (Puerto Rico) came to be. The clouds, mountains, land, sky, and water contain expressive pre-Columbian faces, figurines, and details, thereby evoking the presence of the ancient ancestors throughout the story. This myth of the indigenous people of Boriquén begins with a young boy who collects seeds in his pouch, plants them on top of a mountain, and then watches the results. A forest grows, and a huge flower blooms at the bottom of the tallest tree and then becomes a pumpkin. Two men fight over the pumpkin and its potential power, causing it to break, and out of the pumpkin pours the sea, which rises up to the forest, covering the surrounding land and thus turning the forest into an island. Surrounded by the sea and its creatures, the island is now full of creeks and rivers. The dry existence of the people of Boriquén is over.

Jaffe's text is easily read aloud. Sánchez illustrates the power and beauty of natural elements and complements that power with the wonder and intent of a small boy with a pouch of seeds. Each event is captured in an acrylic and gouache painting that offers both a close-up view and a landscape view. There are rich and varying hues of green and magenta, gold and orange. The blue rivulets and white outlined feathers in the black hair of the characters are especially exquisite. Latinos are multicultural, and this picture book honors and interprets the indigenous heritage of Puerto Ricans in a stunning way. The myth is accessible to all readers, but children ages five to eight will be particularly riveted.

1996
MEDAL WINNER

Soto, Gary. *Chato's Kitchen*. Illustrated by **Susan Guevara**. New York: G. P. Putnam's Sons, 1995.

Chato is a "cool, low-riding cat" from East Los Angeles who discovers that a family of mice has just moved in next door. As he glances through the fence to check out his new neighbors, he scares them out of their wits, for he is the largest cat they have ever laid eyes on. Careful not to alienate the mice, yet eager to eat them for dinner, Chato plays the kind neighbor. He welcomes them to the barrio by asking them over for dinner, sending a paper airplane invitation flying across the fence. Chato invites his best buddy, Novio Boy, his *homes*, to share in his new-found morsels, but not before Novio Boy helps out with the dinner preparations. Together they concoct a delicious home-cooked meal of tortillas, taquitos, enchiladas, chiles rellenos, carne asada, and salsa, served with a fresh pitcher of tamarindo drink and delicious flan for dessert.

The mice, meanwhile, are nervous as they busily prepare to honor their neighbor's invitation. They are about to head out the door when they remember that Chorizo, their dog friend from the old barrio, is coming to their home for dinner that same night, so they invite him to come along to Chato's house. This turns the two cool cats on their heads and foils any attempt to eat the mice. Thus they all manage to enjoy a wonderful Mexican meal.

Guevara's illustrations are a visual feast, brimming with humor and wit as they playfully capture the spirit of East Los Angeles through whimsical, yet symbolic images that abound on every page and serve to authenticate a social and cultural place.

HONOR

Ancona, George. *Pablo Remembers: The Fiesta of the Day of the Dead.* New York: Lothrop, Lee, and Shepard, 1993.

Pablo and his parents and three sisters are a family of weavers from Teotitlán del Valle, Mexico, a small community outside the city of Oaxaca that is famous for its beautiful rugs and weavings. Like most of their fellow Oaxacans, the family participates in *El día de los muertos*, an annual celebration to honor the deceased members of the family.

Days before the feast, Pablo accompanies his parents to the city market, where, along with hundreds of others, they carefully select the best fruits, nuts, vegetables, and *chapulines* (grasshoppers, a delicacy in Oaxaca), the ingredients for a favorite meal they will prepare for Pablo's grandmother, who is recently deceased. They also purchase *pan de muertos*, a special bread made for this feast, small sugar candy skulls, and candles. While at the market, Pablo and his sister observe the bartering and negotiation that takes place between their father and the vendors.

On November 1, the first day of the celebration, the family hustles to complete the many chores that still need to be done. While Pablo's mom makes the *mole*, a traditional Oaxacan meal, his sisters help to prepare the tamales. Pablo and his father, meanwhile, return to the market in search of *Cempasúchil*, the freshly cut, bright orange marigolds used specifically for this celebration. They also buy the sugar cane they will use to construct the arches for the home altar. On November 2, the family participates in the cemetery ritual.

In this striking photo-essay, Ancona—author, photographer, and illustrator—uses sharp color images that alternate between full-page, color close-ups and photo images framed in sections throughout the page. The result is an eloquent story that captures the spirit of a centuries-old tradition and the beauty of a family in the practice of that tradition.

González, Lucía M., reteller. *The Bossy Gallito / El gallo de bodas: A Traditional Cuban Folktale.* Illustrated by **Lulu Delacre**. New York: Scholastic, 1994.

Delacre gives personality to the bossy gallito who is on his way to the wedding of his Tío Perico. The illustrator dresses him in his finest clothes for the wedding and shows the look of puzzlement on his face as the gallito tries to make a decision about two kernels of corn. Temptation gets the better of him, setting in motion his series of panicked cries for help. This delightfully told cumulative Cuban folktale is set in Little Havana, Miami's foremost Cuban neighborhood, known as *la Calle Ocho* (Eighth Avenue). The illustrations accentuate the lush flora and fauna that are typical of the Florida region of the Hispanic Caribbean. In keeping with the wedding theme, Delacre skillfully uses watercolors, colored pencils, and gouache to frame the text and illustrations into oval-shaped portraits. Included are a Spanish glossary to encourage readers to practice the Spanish words and author's and illustrator's notes that add further context to the story and the illustrations.

Lomas Garza, Carmen. *Family Pictures / Cuadros de familia*. San Francisco: Children's Book Press, 1990.

Arturo watches in amazement as his grandmother lays a chicken to eternal rest in preparation for the evening's *caldo* (soup). Margie plays jacks on the kitchen floor as Abuelita makes fresh tortillas and Grandfather prepares a headless rabbit for the family dinner. At a local fund-raiser to benefit the education of Mexican American students, Carmen scribbles on the sidewalk with a twig while her mother helps with the cakewalk and her father serves punch at a GI forum. Mothers, fathers, grandparents, aunts, uncles, *vecinos* (neighbors), and children are all tenderly portrayed in a series of fourteen paintings that together paint a strong story about the cohesiveness of family and community. Whether it is a family outing to the beach or picking oranges in Abuelita's backyard, the paintings detail the routines of daily family and cultural life as experienced by a Mexican American family in South Texas. The scenes are painted from vivid, warm memories and depict the perspective of a loving yet impressionable child. Carmen remembers well the pleasant scenes in these paintings, which serve as a window with a full view into the everyday intricacies, idiosyncrasies, and practices of a strong and nurturing family and community. The colorful paintings are rendered in a naive style, using a mixture of oil on canvas and gouache on arches paper. Each scene is introduced with black-and-white detail constructed by cutting black paper with a craft knife to create *papel picado*.

Biographical Sketches

AUTHORS

2006 Winner
Viola Canales

Viola Canales was born in the border town of McAllen, Texas, in a predominantly Mexican American community. Her barrio consisted of family and friends who were faithful to their religion and their culture. There, *curanderos*, or healers, were commonly consulted; a *curandera* helped clear up an eye infection for Canales when she was a child. Although she could not speak English when she started first grade, Canales learned the language quickly and went on to become an exceptional student.

Photo courtesy of Random House Children's Books

Canales's childhood world was filled with tradition, such as celebrating Day of the Dead and preparing the Christmas *nacimiento*, an elaborate homemade nativity scene. At age fifteen she earned a scholarship to the predominantly white world of St. Stephen's Episcopal boarding school in Austin. It was a dramatic move away from her family and its strong Latino identity. To combat her homesickness, Canales began to write stories about her family and her experiences, some of which appear in *The Tequila Worm*.

Canales is a graduate of Harvard College and Harvard Law School. She was a captain in the U.S. Army and has worked as a community organizer for the United Farm Workers. *The Tequila Worm* is her first novel.

2004 Winner
Julia Alvarez

Photo © by Bill Eichner

In 1960 ten-year-old Julia Alvarez fled the Dominican Republic with her family, very much like twelve-year-old Anita in Alvarez's award-winning book *Before We Were Free*. They left one step ahead of the secret police—for her father, like Anita's, was involved in a plot to overthrow the dictator, Rafael Trujillo. Although Alvarez was born in New York, her family moved back to the Dominican Republic while she was still very young, and they lived in the capital city until their escape in 1960.

At school Alvarez's teachers encouraged her to write about her childhood in the Dominican Republic, and so her path to becoming a writer began. She attended a New England boarding school and then went on to attend Connecticut College in Connecticut, Middlebury College in Vermont, and Syracuse University in New York. In her Pura Belpré acceptance speech, Alvarez said that she was once a migrant writer as she roamed the United States in her little VW. In the course of her writing, she became a poet-in-residence. She also worked in schools, nursing homes, and even prisons.

Of her writing, Alvarez shared the following at the 2004 Pura Belpré Award Ceremony: "We have a tradition in Latin America of *el testimonio*, the testimony, bearing witness. The first step in the awakening of a people's fight for freedom is bearing witness, telling the story of where we have been in order to know where we are going. I wanted to bring young readers into that world of a dictatorship as seen from the eyes of another young person. I wanted young readers to experience firsthand the enormous cost of becoming a free person." Her novels clearly resound with this theme of freedom.

Julia Alvarez is a full-time writer and an award-winning author who spends time in Vermont, where she writes, and in the Dominican Republic, where she remembers the stories told to her by her *tías* and *tíos*, the oral tradition—the gift from her *familia*.

2002 Winner
Pam Muñoz Ryan

Born in Bakersfield, California, on December 25, 1951, award-winning author Pam Muñoz Ryan has written more than twenty-five books for young readers. Because she enjoys variety, her published work includes picture books, novels, and nonfiction. *Esperanza Rising* won not only the Pura Belpré Medal but also the Jane Addams Peace Award and was an Américas Award Honor Book. Her picture-book biography of Marian Anderson, *When Marian Sang*, won the NCTE Orbis Pictus Award and was an ALSC Sibert Honor Book.

Photo courtesy of Scholastic

Ryan grew up in the San Joaquin Valley in a large extended and varied family that enjoyed sharing stories and passing wisdom to the next generation. She found refuge in the library on hot summer days and began her lifelong love of books at that time. After receiving a bachelor's degree from San Diego State University, she worked as an early childhood educator. After she married and began raising her family, Ryan returned to college and received a master's degree, also from San Diego State University. She began by writing books for parents and adults, but found both success and satisfaction when she turned her talent to writing for children and young adults.

She based the story of *Esperanza Rising* on her grandmother, Esperanza Ortega Muñoz, who encountered some of the same struggles in her life as the fictional Esperanza. In her Belpré acceptance speech, Ryan said, "People always ask me why I wrote this book. I wrote this book for two reasons. One, for those that lived before me—my mother and her brothers and sisters. And second, for my children, so that they would know their history."

2000 Winner
Alma Flor Ada

Photo courtesy of Simon and Schuster Children's Publishing

A renowned author, translator, scholar, educator, storyteller, and advocate for multicultural education, Alma Flor Ada was born in Camagüey, Cuba. She spent a lot of time in her backyard communing with nature. The river, animals, and plants all influenced her childhood memories documented in her 2000 Pura Belpré Author Award–winning book, *Under the Royal Palms: A Childhood in Cuba*, a companion book to her previous collection of short stories about her childhood, *Where the Flame Trees Bloom*. In fact, she states, "My grandmother taught me to read before I was three by writing the names of plants and flowers on the earth with a stick."

Ada also spent much of her childhood reading books and listening to the great storytellers in her family, both of which influenced her career. She observes, "Almost all the books I read as a child were translations from other languages, so it isn't surprising that as I grew up I began to translate many books from English into Spanish." Similarly, her grandmother, father, and one of her uncles were all storytellers, which led to Ada's own fondness of storytelling.

After receiving a bachelor's degree from Universidad Central de Madrid in Spain and a master's degree and doctorate from Pontificia Universidad Católica del Peru, Ada did postdoctoral work at Harvard University. She is currently a professor of multicultural education at the University of San Francisco and gives lectures and workshops on the subject throughout the United States.

A prolific writer in both English and Spanish, her work is published in the United States, Spain, Peru, and Argentina. Ada has four children and three grandchildren. One of Ada's children, Rosa Zubizarreta, a writer and translator, often translates her mother's work.

1998 Winner
Victor Martinez

Victor Martinez is a poet, essayist, and short-story writer who was born and raised in the farm worker community of Fresno, California. He was the fourth of twelve children to follow the migrant trail, picking grapes, tomatoes, and peaches. He attended California State University at Fresno as well as Stanford University. He has had many different occupations, including truck driver, office clerk, teacher, fire-fighter, welder, and field laborer. Martinez took the children's publishing world by surprise when he won the 1996 National Book Award in Young People's Literature for *Parrot in the Oven: Mi vida*, his first novel. *Parrot in the Oven* also received the Américas Award and the Boston Globe–Horn Book Honor

Photo by Rubén Guzmán; courtesy of HarperCollins Children's Books

Award. It was also named as one of the New York Public Library's Best Books for Teens. *Parrot in the Oven* has been translated into three other languages: German, French, and Spanish.

1996 Winner
Judith Ortiz Cofer

Photo courtesy of Scholastic

Judith Ortiz Cofer is the first author to win the Pura Belpré Award, and for this reason she holds a place of significance. Being the first was a reciprocal joy and honor for both the first Pura Belpré Award Committee and Ortiz Cofer.

Her book *An Island Like You: Stories of the Barrio* won the first Belpré Author Award, which she accepted at the first REFORMA National Conference, held in Austin, Texas, in 1996. In an interview, Ortiz Cofer reflected, "Winning the award was a great affirmation and source of pride that Latino librarians would acknowledge my work as a contribution."

An Island Like You was her first book for young adults, and the award helped to connect both her and the book to Latino kids all over the country. In her acceptance speech, she noted, "This award will place *An Island Like You* in libraries and make it accessible to large numbers of people. . . . As an educator I have pride in the fact that this award is a seal of approval, that this organization is saying that this book is good enough for the children of America, that my vision is one they want to share."

Born in 1952 in Hormigueros, Puerto Rico, Ortiz Cofer moved to Paterson, New Jersey, when she was two years old. The family maintained direct contact with Puerto Rico, coming and going depending on where her father was stationed as a member of the U.S. Navy. The experience of growing up bilingual and bicultural both on the island and in Paterson provided Ortiz Cofer with rich resources from which to draw. Although first and foremost she is simply called a writer, Ortiz Cofer has also been further classified as "a diasporic Puerto Rican writer, a poet, a multicultural writer, and a multigenre writer."

Influenced by the storytelling women in her family and her poet grandfather, Ortiz Cofer remembers being transported into the world of stories after her grandmother would begin, "*Tengo un cuento.*" Judith Ortiz Cofer is currently the Franklin Professor of English and Creative Writing in the Department of English at the University of Georgia.

A few of her many awards include fellowships from the National Endowment for the Arts, the Witter Bynner Foundation for Poetry, the Florida and Georgia Councils for the Arts, and the Bread Loaf Writers' Conference. In 1998 she received the Albert Christ-Janer Award for creative research and in 1999 was awarded a residency at the Bellagio Study and Conference Center in Italy by the Rockefeller Foundation.

ILLUSTRATORS

2006 Winner
Raúl Colón

Raúl Colón is an acclaimed illustrator of numerous picture books. As a child, he suffered from chronic asthma and frequently had to stay at home for days or weeks at a time. It was during one of these episodes that Colón first learned about a place called the Famous Artists' School and wrote them a letter, only to receive a response saying that he was too young to attend. In high school, he studied art, photography, and commercial art. Colón worked as a commercial artist in New York before moving to Ft. Lauderdale, Florida, where by chance a television company saw his portfolio and hired him to make short films and create puppets for educational programs.

Photo courtesy of Random House Children's Books

Colón's move to New York helped launch his career as an outstanding free-lance artist. His works have appeared in such prestigious publications as the *New York Times*, the *New Yorker*, *Time Magazine*, and the *Wall Street Journal*. His artwork has also been commissioned for theater posters, annual reports, and advertisements. He is highly regarded for his distinctive style of work, which consists of expressive compositions that employ watercolor and colored pencil.

He has received Gold and Silver medals from the Society of Illustrators for his contributions to outstanding illustration. For *Doña Flor*, he received the Society of Children's Book Writers and Illustrators Golden Kite Award.

2004 Winner
Yuyi Morales

Photo courtesy Yuyi Morales

Yuyi Morales was born in the city of flowers, Xalapa, Mexico, to parents Eloina and Eligio. She spent the first twenty-five years of her life in Mexico, where she took an early interest in drawing and sports. As an adolescent, she showed promise as a competitive swimmer and enrolled at the University of Xalapa, where she earned a bachelor's degree in physical education and psychology.

Morales says that Mexico is her *corazón*, her heart. In 1994 she moved to the United States with her husband and son and started experimenting with puppet making. In 1997 she created a weekly children's radio program for KPOO of San Francisco. Drawing from the legends and myths of Latin America, the show ran for three years. At that same time she began writing and illustrating her own children's stories.

In 2000 the Society of Children's Book Writers and Illustrators (SCBWI) awarded Morales the Don Freeman Memorial Grant-in-Aid for her work in illustration. Three years later her first book, *Harvesting Hope: The Story of César Chávez*, by Kathleen Krull, appeared in print and won the Christopher Award, the Jane Addams Award, a Pura Belpré Honor Book Award, and an Américas Award Honorable Mention. *Harvesting Hope* was also prized as one of the best books of 2003 by publications such as *Child* magazine, the *San Francisco Chronicle*, *School Library Journal*, and *Booklist*.

About her Pura Belpré Award, Morales had this to say, "I want to stop to say how honored I am to have won an award chosen and given by librarians. I am especially thrilled because the Pure Belpré Award gave me the perfect opportunity to come declare in the open my infatuation with the public library." The 2004 Illustrator Award winner for *Just a Minute: A Trickster Tale and Counting Book*, Morales was also awarded the 2004 Illustrator Honor Award for *Harvesting Hope: The Story of César Chávez*, by Kathleen Krull. An ALA Notable Book, *Just a Minute* is also the recipient of the Américas Award and numerous others, including a Parents' Choice Seal of Approval and a Golden Kite Honor Book.

Yuyi Morales lives in the San Francisco Bay Area with her husband and son.

2002 and 1996 Winner
Susan Guevara

Susan Guevara is a two-time Pura Belpré Medal winner. She was the recipient of the first Pura Belpré Illustrator Award in 1996 for *Chato's Kitchen* and followed that honor in 2002 with another Belpré Medal for *Chato and the Party Animals*. In 2005 the third book about Chato and his friends, *Chato Goes Cruisin'*, was published, adding to a long line of books illustrated in a variety of styles by Guevara.

Photo courtesy of Penguin Young Readers Group

Guevara was born in Walnut Creek, California, and currently lives in New Mexico, where she divides her time between book illustration and painting. Her art has been heavily influenced by her studies in Belgium and France. However, she has recently become more involved in studying the symbolism and magical realism of native Mexican art. She has a bachelor of fine arts from San Francisco Art Academy.

Guevara uses her art to meld the beauty and wonder of the world with her Mexican heritage. It is easy to see that the many symbols found in the art of Mexican folk artists and Chicano muralists have influenced Guevara's work in both *Chato's Kitchen* and *Chato and the Party Animals*.

2000 Winner
Carmen Lomas Garza

Photo courtesy of Children's
Book Press

The 1996 Pura Belpré Illustrator Honor Award winner for *Family Pictures / Cuadros de familia*, the 1998 Pura Belpré Illustrator Honor Award winner for *In My Family / En mi familia*, and the 2000 Pura Belpré Illustrator Award winner for *Magic Windows / Ventanas mágicas*, Carmen Lomas Garza was born in Kingsville, Texas, in 1948. These three books draw heavily from her childhood memories of living near the Mexican border with her family. Lomas Garza's mother was her first art teacher, from whom she learned many crafts or *artesanias* (traditional folk art). Similarly, her grandmother taught her to make *papel picado* (paper cutouts), the subject of her Pura Belpré Award–winning book. At the age of thirteen, Lomas Garza decided to become a visual artist.

Lomas Garza earned a bachelor of science from Texas Arts and Industry University in Kingsville, Texas, in 1972; a master of education from Juarez-Lincoln/Antioch Graduate School in Austin, Texas, in 1973; and a master of art from San Francisco State University in San Francisco, California, in 1981. Inspired by the Chicano Movement of the late 1960s, the artist has chosen to "create images that would elicit recognition and appreciation among Mexican Americans, both adults and children, while at the same time, serve as a source of education for others not familiar with our culture. It has been my objective since 1969 to make paintings, prints, installations for Day of the Dead, paper and metal cutouts that instill pride in our history and culture in American society."

Currently living in San Francisco, California, Lomas Garza is the recipient of numerous awards, including the Américas Award and the Tomás Rivera Mexican American Children's Book Award. Her work has been displayed in both individual and group exhibitions in museums throughout the world, such as the Smithsonian Institution in Washington, D.C., the Whitney Museum of American Art in New York City, and the Mexican Museum in San Francisco, California.

1998 Winner
Stephanie Garcia

Stephanie Garcia was born in Los Angeles, California, and spent most of her growing years in the Montebello area just outside East Los Angeles. Her father is a second generation Mexican American with family ties to the famed Mexican agrarian leader Emiliano Zapata. Her mother is a first generation Mexican American who grew up in El Paso, Texas, in abject poverty.

Photo courtesy of Stephanie Garcia

As a child Garcia loved to paint, drawing and painting on every surface available to her. She credits her parents for nurturing her creativity at such a young age; she was only three and a half years old when her father built her a mini workbench, complete with work and art tools and stocked with a variety of paints and crayons.

It was during her high school years, however, that Garcia began to create her own images to complement the stories she was reading in her textbooks. Upon her graduation from Schurr High School in Montebello, she applied to the Art Center College of Design in Pasadena, California, but was not initially accepted. She was so determined to become an artist, however, that she applied a second time, that time receiving a merit scholarship. She graduated with the highest honor of distinction.

A master of three-dimensional works of art, she first draws up her preliminary plans in sketches and then, using various media, creates carpentry work based on these sketches. After much rearrangement, she photographs the works of art and reduces the photos to create a final piece. *Snapshots from the Wedding*, which received the Pura Belpré Award in 1998, was done in this manner. She is, however, comfortable with many different art forms and is currently exploring the use of large canvases.

In 2004 Garcia was selected as one of ten outstanding artists to mentor aspiring artists in the design and arts profession, focusing on social responsibility. The mentoring position is sponsored by W. K. Kellogg Foundation and is a project of Worldstudio, which is based in New York City.

Garcia lives with her husband, Jonathan, in Hoboken, New Jersey.

Part II

Booktalks

for the Author Award Books

2006
MEDAL WINNER

The Tequila Worm, by Viola Canales

When Doña Clara pulled out her jar full of big mule teeth, Sofia's first thought was, "Oh no! Please don't say I inherited those teeth too!" She'd already been told that she had inherited her great-great-grandmother's gift for mule-kicking. But Clara did not point to Sofia. Instead, she pointed to Berta.

This book is filled with moments rich in family tradition, the Mexican American way. For example, the author describes how Sofia and Berta along with Sofia's little sister, Lucy, and Berta's little brother, Noe, used to practice First Communion. Sofia would take a roll of Necco candy wafers, pull out the white ones, and place them in a yellow cup. Then they would practice communion until the white wafers were gone. (Sofia would eat all the rest!)

Stories of *cascarones*, Berta's *quinceañera*, Day of the Dead, and the Christmas *nacimiento* fill out the chapters. When Sofia wins a scholarship to an elite boarding school in Austin called Saint Luke's, each family member reacts differently. Sofia is determined to go, and she gets a part-time job sorting cucumbers from a moving conveyor belt to help pay for her expenses. As the start of school gets closer, Sofia realizes that she will need five decent dresses for the dinner meals at the school. A quick trip to Johnson's Ropa Usada turns into an afternoon of sorting through mountains of clothes to find them.

Although the scholarship to Saint Luke's provides Sofia with wonderful opportunities, it takes her from her family and the Latino culture that has surrounded her for her entire life. Read about Sofia's trials, adventures, embarrassments, and more—and find out about the glow-in-the-dark rosary, the panty-hose baby, and of course, the tequila worm.

HONOR

César: ¡Sí, Se Puede! Yes, We Can! by Carmen T. Bernier-Grand

Many words have been written about César Chávez, the organizer of the United Farm Workers, whose efforts led to better working conditions for those who harvest some of the fresh vegetables and fruits that come to our tables. But this book is different. Not only does it tell about César's hard work but also his life growing up and as a young man. It tells his story in the form of poems that describe in just a few words the actions that meant so much. David Diaz illustrated this book using his computer. The illustrations seem to glow with an inner light and with the soft but vibrant colors that Californians see in the fields as the crops are growing. This book won the Pura Belpré Award for its illustrations, but it was also honored for its words. Read this book twice—once by reading the words and once just by looking at the pictures. It will be a double treat!

Doña Flor: A Tall Tale about a Giant Woman with a Great Big Heart, by Pat Mora

Have you ever seen a flower grow? They say that if you sing to flowers, they grow. Well, that is exactly what Flor's *mamá* did when Flor was a little baby. Her *mamá* sang lovely songs and lullabies in a sweet voice. In fact, she sang to Flor so much that, well . . . Flor just kept on growing. Flor grew so big and tall! Why, she even had such gigantic feet that the other children called her Big Foot. Why, she was so tall that when the wind grew restless, Flor would just hug Father Wind and that would calm him down.

Flor learned to speak many different languages. She was known to be able to speak to her tiny creature friends like the butterflies and the grasshoppers. Why, they say she even spoke rattler. Can you speak rattler? Let's speak rattler just for a second now. . . .

Now back to our story. Flor became so big and so tall that soon the children of the village where she grew up began to ask her for *favores* . . . that's "favors" in Spanish. It's spelled almost the same. "Por favor," they would say. "Flor, can you give us a ride?" This big woman with the big feet and the big body soon began to help all the children and grown-ups in her *pueblito*, in her small village. Children loved to "ride" to school on Flor's enormous body. The children also loved to visit Doña Flor in her home, which was like a forest filled with the most beautiful flowers and plants. Everything imaginable grew in her garden: poppies, morning glories, roses, sunflowers, tomatoes, and even chiles. Flor was so good and so kind to everyone that soon all the people in the pueblo began to call her Doña Flor because they respected her so much.

But one day, the children from the pueblo failed to show up for Doña Flor's storytime. So Flor decided to do some investigating. It turned out that the people in the village were frightened by a loud roaring sound coming from the other side of the canyon. The village people ran to Doña Flor, who quickly discovered that . . . Well, that, dear boys and girls, is exactly what you will have to discover when you read this charming story of the big and beautiful woman Doña Flor, whose heart and spirit are as enormous as she is.

Becoming Naomi León, by Pam Muñoz Ryan

Naomi likes to make lists. She has lists of "Splendid Words" and "Unusual Names." But Naomi keeps other lists as well, like "Things That Were the Good and the Bad All Rolled into One." This list includes "1) We had a trailer so we lived real simple without a lot of stuff, 2) We had avocados growing nearby and could eat as many as we wanted to the point of getting sick, 3) Gram was an expert seamstress and made all of our clothes out of polyester-blend remnants, and 4) Gram was retired and could devote her every waking moment to me and Owen." Then she has to add "Our mother came back" to the list. Naomi and her brother Owen don't know what to think when their mother reappears after being away for seven years. They love Gram, but they have longed for their mother and a real family. But then Skyla, their mother, begins to show them what living with her would really be like. And they are not sure they like it.

2004
MEDAL WINNER

Before We Were Free, by Julia Alvarez

If you were twelve, how would you feel if soldiers with guns barged into your home and started going through all your possessions? How would you react if your favorite lamp lay broken on the ground? What kind of questions would you ask your parents? Would you feel safe in your home? Whom could you trust?

The place is the Dominican Republic. The time is the 1960s. The ruler is General Rafael Trujillo, a terrifying dictator. It is a time of fear and uncertainty for all. For twelve-year-old Anita, it is also a time of confusion. What is happening to her family? How can her mother expect her to be brave and strong when she cannot even understand what is happening? Not even Chucha, the family's housekeeper, will answer her questions.

Chucha has been part of the de la Torre family for a very long time, and she likes to remind Anita that she was the one who changed Anita's diapers. (How embarrassing!) Chucha only wears purple (even her underwear is dyed purple), and she sleeps in a coffin—yes, a coffin—by which she says she is preparing herself for the next life. As strange as that behavior may seem, Anita feels very safe with Chucha.

When you are going on thirteen years old, thoughts of boys are not far away, and when the Washburns moved into the de la Torre family compound, along came Sam with hair so blond it looked almost white. Sam and Anita became instant friends, exploring the compound together. But why did he tell her, "See you later, alligator"? Alligators are such ugly animals, aren't they?

But then a scary thing happens. The secret police, called the SIM, raid the de la Torre compound, breaking many of the family's possessions and even overturning Chucha's coffin. Anita is warned not to mention the raid to anyone. But why did the SIM raid her home? Why did they break her things? When Anita overhears her father and his friends speaking quietly below her bedroom window, she discovers that her father is part of a plot to assassinate Trujillo. What will happen to her family? Will the plot work? Will life ever be free of fear for Anita and her family?

Before We Were Free takes readers on a fast-paced journey. Julia Alvarez's words evoke the fear and uncertainly that pervaded the Dominican Republic during General Trujillo's regime. The terrifying events are fictionalized but based on an actual time and place in the Dominican Republic's bloody history.

HONOR

Cuba 15, by Nancy Osa

Have you ever been told that you had to do something you didn't want to do? What was your reaction? Did you feel upset or irritated? Did you feel that life was unfair, or did you accept what you were told to do as a challenge?

Violet Paz is having a party, but it's not of her choosing, and she is not sure she will survive it. According to her Cuban grandmother, Violet must celebrate her entry into womanhood with a traditional birthday celebration called a *quinceañera*, or *quince* for short. But what is a *quinceañera*? Do you have to be Cuban to have one? What exactly happens at a *quince* party? And why should she have one? After all, she's already been fifteen for a whole week, her mother is Polish, and she has green eyes and almost blond hair. She doesn't even look Cuban. So what's the big deal? Her best friends, Janell and Leda, think the idea of a *quince* is cool and have agreed to be *damas de honor*, part of Anita's honor court. After all, they won't have to stand on stage and give speeches. What would be your reaction to giving a speech in front of family and friends?

Although the thought of the *quince* is living with her night and day, Violet has other dilemmas to solve. What will she prepare for her school speech competition? Her category is comedy, and the subject matter must be appropriate and must not include any swearing. When her *abuela*'s idea to have a barbeque for potential sponsors of Violet's *quinceañera* results in chaos, Violet has the material for her speech. Who wouldn't enjoy hearing about Grandfather, the roast on fire, and the booming voice of Tía Sara chanting, "Cha-cha-cha, cha-cha-cha"?

Colorful characters parade through this book, including Abuelo, who is from Miami and loves a good game of dominoes; Papi, who never wants to discuss Cuba; Leda, a teen activist and Violet's good friend; and Chucho, the dog who looks like a little old man with an extra pair of legs and a tail.

My Diary from Here to There / Mi diario de aquí hasta allá, by Amada Irma Pérez

Have you ever moved to a new home? Do you know anyone who has? Do you know what it feels like to be the new person in school? "Dear Diary" begins this story of one young girl's fears as she overhears her parents whisper about moving. And this isn't a move down the street or to a nearby neighborhood. This isn't a move into a new city or new state. It is all of these things and more. Young Amada and her family are moving out of their home, out of their neighborhood, out of their city, out of their state, and out of their country. They are moving from Mexico to the United States.

But how can that be? Amada is certain that her brothers will be upset when they find out. Instead, they are excited and can't wait to see the big stores that sell all kinds of toys. Is Amada the only one who is scared of leaving? What will happen if she isn't allowed to speak Spanish in the United States? And what will happen if she can't learn to speak English?

Have you ever wondered what it would be like to speak a new language? Do you think it would be difficult to learn? How long do you think it would take for you to learn a new language? If you had to move and all you could take were a few of your things, what would you choose?

This story is written in both English and Spanish, and Amada Irma Pérez invites the reader into the journey her family made many years ago, when she was the young Amada feeling the uncertainty of moving to a new place. In her notes Amada writes that she was five years old when her family left Juárez, Mexico, for their new life in Los Angeles, California. Enjoy the ride, and experience Amada's conflicting feelings of longing for Mexico and then joy as she realizes that Mexico will always be in her memories and in her heart.

2002
MEDAL WINNER

Esperanza Rising, by Pam Muñoz Ryan

Life was perfect for Esperanza Ortega. She lived in comfort as the pampered daughter of a rich landowner in Mexico. Esperanza learns a love of the land from her beloved *papá*, and she learns how to be a lady from her beautiful *mamá*. Her *abuela* (her grandmother) teaches her needlework and patience. She eagerly awaits her thirteenth birthday, knowing that it too will be perfect.

However, on the eve of her birthday, Esperanza's *papá* is murdered and she and her family go into a tailspin. Mamá refuses to marry again, and out of spite their home is burned and their ranch is destroyed. What is left for Esperanza, her mother, and her grandmother? Where can they turn for help?

Esperanza means *hope* in Spanish, and that is all that Esperanza and her mother have left. With their former servants, they travel to California to work in the fields as *campesinas*. What do you think is the hardest thing Esperanza has to learn in her life? Is it sweeping floors? Changing diapers? Working as a day laborer? Not having pretty things? Or empathy for others who don't have nice things?

Esperanza must be strong for her mother. And she must have faith in the future. Her thirteenth year is long and challenging. As the crops change with the seasons, Esperanza changes with her new experiences, finding new strength within herself. And in the end she learns that *esperanza* comes from family and friends, from the land, and from patience.

HONOR

Iguanas in the Snow and Other Winter Poems / Iguanas en la nieve y otros poemas de invierno, by Francisco X. Alarcón

What do you think of when you think of winter? Many people think first of snow, cold, and gray days. *Iguanas in the Snow* captures some of those feelings with poems such as "Winter Sun," which begins,

brother Sun—
I haven't seen you
in many days

Poems like this one help create a mood, but they also make you see a picture in your mind of gray days that never seem to end. And they make you remember what it is like to want to see the sun again.

In *Iguanas in the Snow*, Alarcón's poems create a mood and also create pictures in your mind. His poems are set in San Francisco and the Bay Area in California. With just a few words in each poem, he describes unique sites like the famous sea lions on Pier 39 and the giant sequoias that tourists enjoy. But he also highlights the everyday things, such as the neighborhood school. He describes his cousin Rocking Rafael, a cable car conductor. Rafael hums old rock and roll songs as he runs the cable car and dances in the rain. Alarcón writes about the Misión de Dolores, the oldest building in the Mission District. The poet says its walls keep you warm, "just like my grandma's broad arms."

These poems are written in both English and Spanish. Can you guess what the poem, "Primera Nevada" means in English? This small poem illustrates the feeling you get when you watch the snow falling. The English translation of the title is "First Snowfall."

But the title of this book, *Iguanas in the Snow*, is a puzzle, isn't it? Have you ever seen iguanas playing in the snow? We think about iguanas living in hot deserts, don't we? If you want to find out what the iguanas in the snow are, you will have to read this book. But have a nice cup of hot chocolate handy, because you may feel a cold blast of winter when you read these poems!

Breaking Through, by Francisco Jiménez

"I was getting ready to recite the preamble to the Declaration of Independence, which our class had to memorize. . . . After the bell rang, my teacher was interrupted by a knock on the door. As soon as I saw the green uniform, I panicked. Miss Ehlis and the officer walked up to me. 'Are you Francisco Jiménez?' he asked."

Thus begins Francisco's long journey to break through the poverty and other barriers in his life. Francisco's story is about his yearning to enjoy the promises given to American citizens in the Declaration of Independence. He and his family strive to enjoy life, liberty, and the pursuit of happiness and to feel equal to others, but it doesn't come easily.

How many of you think you have too many chores to do at home? Eighth-grader Francisco and his sixteen-year-old brother Roberto had to live by themselves while their family tried to save enough money to return to California to work. Each day before they went to school, Francisco and Roberto made their own breakfast, made their beds, swept the floor, and washed the dishes. After school and on weekends they worked in the fields picking crops or at their jobs as janitors. Then they came home, made their own supper, and cleaned up. *And* they had to study each night just like you do.

But it was harder for Francisco and his family. They were still learning English and the customs in America. And they were struggling to earn enough money to feed a growing family. Francisco knew that the best way to get ahead was to get a good education, so he tried every day to stay at the top of his class.

How does someone from a background like Francisco's become a top student in his school while working every day to help support his family? How does someone from a poor immigrant family who began school not knowing any English graduate from high school with scholarships so he can go to college? *Breaking Through* is based on the true story of Francisco Jiménez. It is the sequel to *The Circuit*, which tells the story of Francisco's life from the time he is a small boy until he is in junior high. It is a story of hope, hard work, and helping hands along the way.

2000
MEDAL WINNER

Under the Royal Palms: A Childhood in Cuba, by Alma Flor Ada

Alma Flor Ada grew up on the Caribbean island called Cuba. *Under the Royal Palms* is the story of her childhood there, where she lived with her extended family in a house built during colonial times. Every day Ada would be awakened by the smell of coffee. All the adult members of the family, except Ada's mother, would be preparing to leave the house for the day. Ada would spend her day playing until late afternoon, then she would take a bath and dress for dinner. After dinner, she and her grandmother would settle on the porch and wait for the first bats to appear. The bats lived above the porch and weren't seen or heard during the day except for the occasional young one that would accidentally fall from its roost.

Ada's days, like those of many in her city, were calm and routine. So when something out of the ordinary happened, it stuck in her mind, perhaps more than it would have if things hadn't normally been so calm. She speculates that perhaps that is why her memories are so vivid now.

Have you ever had a secret? Ada had one. She admired her Uncle Medardo, who wanted to fly an airplane even though no one in the family wanted him to do it. But he bought his own plane and would fly it on weekends whenever he could. Although the rest of the family disapproved, Ada secretly admired her uncle. One day the sky cleared after a dark and cloudy morning. Medardo was determined to fly, but his plane crashed in Ada's backyard and he lost his life. Though her father tried to shield her, he could not prevent Ada from seeing the tragic event. It was a tremendous loss for the entire family. Medardo left behind a widow and an infant daughter. Ada, a young child, felt guilty and so did something that she has kept secret until now.

Ada's uncle was not her only loss. When she transferred to a new school, she was very unhappy. One day she peeked into the ballet school nearby and joined the class. She became close to the ballet teacher. But tragedy struck once more when the teacher collapsed mid-recital and eventually died of the cancer that had caused her collapse.

Through good times and bad, Ada's family always had each other. Like the royal palms in the book's title, which stand majestically over Cuba, Ada's family stood tall under all circumstances.

HONOR

From the Bellybutton of the Moon and Other Summer Poems / Del ombligo de la luna y otros poemas de verano, by Francisco X. Alarcón

Think about your summer vacations. What do you normally do? When Francisco Alarcón was a boy, his entire family drove to Mexico to visit his grandmother in the town where she was raised. They drove through Mexico's western mountain range, the Sierra Madre Occidental. "The golden eyeglasses of my father / the windshield of my family's station wagon." Does that sound like long car trips you have taken with your family?

Once they arrived, Francisco and his brothers and sisters got to spend time with their grandmother and other relatives. Auntie Reginalda makes "delicious breakfasts / little yellow suns / smiling in our plates." His Uncle Vicente says, "tomorrow / we'll start / all over" after he has spent the day farming. He and his siblings learn the Spanish alphabet from Grandpa Pancho.

The children spend a lot of time outside with nature. They spend time in the ocean, in the grass, and in the trees. Francisco names his favorite cow Mariposa—the Spanish word for *butterfly*. He names her Mariposa "because she has the mark of a butterfly on her face." He imagines that "perhaps more than a cow she really is a butterfly!" Playing outside puts a lot of wear and tear on one's shoes. The poet acknowledges their role in "Ode to My Shoes": "my shoes rest all night under my bed / . . . / and wake up cheerful relaxed so soft."

Just saying "Mexico" brings the town of Atoyac, where Francisco spent his summers, to his senses: "I feel the same wind on my face / . . . / I see Atoyac again / . . . / I hear familiar voices / . . . / I smell my grandma's gardenias." In another poem, Francisco hears his "grandma telling me / about the Aztecs." He writes,

"Mexico" says my grandma
"means: from the bellybutton of the moon"
"don't forget your origin my son"
maybe that's why
whenever I now say "Mexico"
I feel like touching my bellybutton.

His grandfather's Spanish alphabet lessons and his annual visits to Mexico probably helped the poet maintain his bilingual skills as he is now an accomplished bilingual poet, educator, and translator. He has also written three companion books to this one, which contain poems about the three other seasons. But the family's bilingual skills are not limited to people, as is illustrated in the poem "Bilingual," where the bilingual dog barks, "*guau guau*" in Spanish and then, "bowwow" in English.

Laughing Out Loud, I Fly: Poems in English and Spanish, by Juan Felipe Herrera

What makes you laugh? How does it sound when you laugh at a joke that wasn't very funny but you felt that you had to laugh anyway? How does it sound when you are watching a really funny movie? Have any of you started laughing with a friend for no reason? Maybe you just looked at each other, started laughing, and couldn't stop no matter how hard you tried? How does laughing that hard make you feel? Can you explain why that happens? Can you describe it? Do you think we can call it playing?

In *Laughing Out Loud, I Fly: Poems in English and Spanish*, the poet, Juan Felipe Herrera, wanted to write poems about his childhood. He wanted to play. But he wanted to play with words. He also wanted to look at things differently and try to include that different way of looking in his poetry. So he started playing, putting all the words in these poems together. He wanted the playing to make him laugh out loud. He wanted to laugh out loud so hard that it would make him fly.

These poems bring back to life memories of his childhood by describing various events, food, toys, and people. The poet also looked at things differently by including in the poems whatever came to mind and made him laugh. In the first poem, "Laughing Out Loud, I Fly," Herrera writes,

> I am a monkey cartoon or a chile *tamal*, crazy
> with paisley patches, infinite flavors cinnamon &
> banana ice cream, it's 3 in the afternoon, no, at 5
> my mother says she will call me
> & arrive, a rainbow.

Is he really a monkey cartoon or banana ice cream? No. But he is playing and trying to make himself laugh by thinking he is a monkey cartoon.

In "I Own Many Socks, Some with Wings," he writes, "'Where are my sockos?' as Papi says / one tambourine socko for your flower-vase head." In Spanish the lines rhyme even better, and you don't even need to understand Spanish to hear the rhyme: "'*Dónde están mis calcetas?' como dice Papi, / una calceta de pandereta para tu maceta.*" Here's another rhyme: "The enchilada the butcher gave me / was filled with split peas & indigo, a crazy red train, you believe me?"

It seems that he includes all that comes to mind as he tries to see the world differently. For example:

> I count dry chile vines & ancient leaves, count count
> a Mexico in Los Angeles, giant Oaxaca in tiny Alaska,
> this autumn fiesta torn to pieces, well, let's count:
> 123 & 8910, is this a story about rice or is it rice with milk?

Here are the titles of some of his other poems: "Chico, the Smallest, Just Like This, Chico"; "When the Mail Carrier Discovered My Aunt"; "Nothing Is Missing, Nothing, Except the Pineapple Tamales"; and "I Wake Again with a Sesame Seed & a Green-Headed Pea." What are they about? You'll have to read the book to find out!

1998
MEDAL WINNER

Parrot in the Oven: Mi vida, by Victor Martinez

Do you know what it means to live in the projects? Do you or does anyone you know live in the projects? When you think of the projects, can you describe who might live there?

Fourteen-year-old Manny Hernandez is a compassionate observer of the hardships of his family life in the projects. When entering Manny's world, some teenage readers will find the circumstances familiar. Others will find insight into the life of a friend or cousin or even someone they will meet later in life.

Despite his father's fierce pride, Manny would like to see his father with a job again, drinking less, and controlling his rage. He would love at the least to see his mother get the new coat that she has been admiring and even more so to see her leave his father. But, for now, he is the family facilitator. He looks out for his two sisters, he tries to stop the domestic violence, and he cajoles his older brother into working smart while picking chile peppers or making deliveries for the pharmacy—often without reward or recognition.

It is not always easy to feel safe and happy when there are problems in your own home. Can Manny prevent his father's rage? What would you do if you were Manny? Would you feel helpless? Angry? Would these troubling circumstances make you stronger?

Outside of his home, Manny is coming of age—as all teenagers do. There are peer pressures, and he is discovering girls. In Manny's neighborhood, however, there are other, more serious issues that he must deal with. For one, he must deal with questionable and strained relationships with the white neighbors, other teens, and his teachers. He also must choose whether or not to join a gang in order to relieve boredom and survive more easily in the streets. He even encounters prejudice from his own Mexican American community, as when he takes his sister to the hospital on the bus. These challenges are draining, but he bounces back. Sometimes you might feel that others judge you by how you look, how you dress, by the color of your skin, and more. Have you ever felt this way? How did you react?

Victor Martinez, as the narrative voice of Manny, plunges into the use of imagery, metaphors, and *dichos* (Mexican sayings) to express his soul. Readers of Latino heritage will recognize the sayings that are often repeated by someone in the family to offer lessons on life and living. Using vignettes, Martinez offers various scenes from Manny's daily life. They are not sweet scenes but rather very real depictions of teenage worries, fears, and hopes that come with the effort to survive emotionally and physically. Still, Manny has a spirit of integrity and rugged individuality that keeps the reader interested and concerned. Readers might enjoy discussing whether Manny truly is a "parrot in the oven" as his father suggests. What do you think? Is Manny a parrot in the oven?

HONOR

Laughing Tomatoes and Other Spring Poems / Jitomates risueños y otros poemas de primavera, by Francisco X. Alarcón

Have you ever thought of becoming a poet or a painter? You can bring your thoughts or ideas to life through word pictures or actual paintings and drawings. And if you speak more than one language, you have so many more ways to express yourself!

Take a look at *Laughing Tomatoes / Jitomates risueños*. Francisco Alarcón has written his poems in English and Spanish, and Maya Christina Gonzalez has painted her interpretations of the poems—what they mean to her. Poems do not have to be long. Take a look at "First Rain / *Primera lluvia*," for instance:

is it raining
or
is the sky crying?

*¿llueve
o
llora
el cielo?*

For this poem, Gonzalez painted an *abuelita* holding an umbrella with one hand and petting her dog with the other, while above her is a huge cloud with its eyes closed, weeping raindrops.

We can use poetry to learn or teach about holidays. Here is part of the poem titled "Cinco de Mayo":

a battle
in some
history books
a fiesta
of music
and colors . . .

and in Spanish:

*una batalla
en los libros
de historia
una fiesta
de música
y colores*

How do you recognize Cinco de Mayo? Gonzalez paints a scene of a blindfolded *abuelita* trying to hit a huge, colorful piñata. There is also a table with bowls of corn chips, guacamole, and *pan dulce*. The colors—pink, turquoise, and gold—are bright. The dogs in the scene are smiling. What colors do you like? How does the color red make you feel?

A poem can tell a story. It can also be your imagination written down. Can you picture a tomato laughing? Alarcón can:

with joy
they grow round
with flavor
laughing
they change
to red

Can you imagine strawberries as "*dulces / tiernos / corazones*," or in English as "sweet / tender / hearts"?

After reading *Laughing Tomatoes*, you will be inspired to write about your own favorite fruits, holidays, people, and day-to-day observations—or maybe even your dreams!

Spirits of the High Mesa, by Floyd Martinez

People usually say that change is good, but one thing is for sure: change is nearly unstoppable most of the time. Change can occur very quickly, or it can occur slowly. Imagine that you have new technology in your city that changes the way you work, cook, read, or watch TV. Electricity is one example. We already have some wireless capability, but we still depend on electrical outlets for most things. Can you imagine life without them? You would perhaps have a faster way to turn appliances on, but it would be *totally* different from what you are used to. It would take time to adjust, wouldn't it? And remember that one change causes many other changes. Maybe new people planning to take jobs created by the new technology would be moving into your neighborhood in large numbers. Perhaps you would find yourself in a whole new world. What are the pros and cons of change?

Flavio, the main character in *Spirits of the High Mesa*, used to work and play by candlelight or starlight until electricity came to his small village. He was excited to have heat without having to chop wood all the time to make fires to warm up, cook, or heat water. He worked hard with every season as his grandfather, El Grande, taught him. But his grandfather, respectful of wildlife and nature, was not happy about the changes. They upset his routine, his traditions, and what he felt were the customs of the village. Flavio had a special bond with his grandfather and felt torn about his loyalty. His mother and most of the women in the village were excited about the changes. Have you ever felt caught in the middle? Have you ever been afraid of being disloyal or being a traitor because you were excited about something that another person was not? How did you handle it? Do you have a close relationship with one of your grandparents or aunts or uncles or maybe a *niño* or *niña*? Why is it special? Have you had to say good-bye to this person? What was the reason?

El Grande taught Flavio how to approach wildlife and nature with respect. He taught Flavio not to cut down a tree or hunt an animal needlessly. There had to be a good reason to do either of these things, and no part of the tree or the animal should be wasted. What are some of the ways that we are wasteful with the Earth or take too much from it? How could we do better? Are there any good things we are doing to protect the Earth, even with change and progress?

Spirits of the High Mesa provides insight into what it is like to live on a *rancho* in a rural Native American and Hispanic community. There are some funny characters, such as Lorenzo, the "ape-kid" with long arms, and Tuls, the kid from Oklahoma. There are characters who may be familiar to some of us, like Malvino, the man who seems a little crazy although no one really knows for sure. There is also Mrs. Majors, who is very strict and sometimes seems to favor certain kids. Every community has a cast of characters, but maybe that is what makes a community. What do you think?

1996
MEDAL WINNER

An Island Like You: Stories of the Barrio, by Judith Ortiz Cofer

La mala influencia—it sounds like a disease. What do you think it means? Do you think you have ever had it?

Rita is a blossoming, sassy young teen who lives with her parents in the tenement building known as El Building in Paterson, New Jersey. She and her girlfriend Meli each tell their parents that they are spending the night at the other's house, but the plot is foiled when Meli's little sister reveals that they have gone to Joey Molieri's house. Rita is placed under house arrest before being shipped off to "the island," Puerto Rico, to live with her grandparents for the summer. Expecting to serve out her sentence in utter boredom, Rita actually learns to appreciate her grandparents and their way of life, replete with household roosters and weird motions used as spiritual healings for *mala influencia*.

Now, I am sure that you have never been sneaky and made up a story to cover your tracks, have you? Do you know if any of your friends have ever said they were going to be one place when they really planned to be somewhere else? If you were shipped off to stay with your grandparents for the summer, what do you think would happen? Would you have a good time?

This is a book filled with short stories, but they are all sort of interconnected. Everyone in the stories lives in the same building. Have you ever lived in an apartment or tenement building? What do you think living in an apartment or tenement building is like? In one of the stories, the elderly residents of the tenement building mistake Arturo for a punk because he spikes his purple hair. When his parents reprimand him, he grows furious and decides to leave home. In haste he pulls out his meager savings and mistakenly throws "Willy" Shakespeare into the dumpster. While seeking solace at St. Joseph's Church, his conversation with the old church keeper, Johann, reignites his love for poetry and literature. He returns to the dumpster to learn which poem his friend Kenny will be reciting for the next day's class.

These and other carefully crafted stories provide vivid yet subtle portraits of young Puerto Rican teenagers who are connected to one another and live as neighbors, classmates, and residents in El Building. The stories create a landscape of the lives of impressionable teens as they wrestle with a variety of cultural and social issues while in search of their own identities.

HONOR

The Bossy Gallito / El gallo de bodas: A Traditional Cuban Folktale, by Lucía M. González

Have you ever been in a situation where you get all dressed up but are so nervous about being on time that you find you can't do much of anything? You become almost paralyzed, unable to do anything at all. Such is the case with the main character, Señor Rooster, in this delightful story, *The Bossy Gallito*. Señor Rooster is excited because his Tío Perico's wedding day has arrived. The *gallito* got himself all dressed up, looking ever so elegant. But in all the excitement of the wedding, he forgot to grab a bite to eat. Soon he is quite hungry, but he does not dare eat because he knows that if he eats his beak will get dirty, and he cannot afford to show up at his uncle's wedding with a dirty beak. Besides, a dirty beak does not go with his elegant attire.

Poor rooster, he finds himself in quite a big dilemma. Soon hunger gets the best of him, and sure enough, next thing you know, he dirties his beak as he feasts on two kernels of corn he finds by the side of the road. What would you do if you were in such a bind? I bet you would do exactly as the *gallito* in this story did. I bet you would go and ask your friends for help. But how you ask for help makes the difference between getting help and not getting any help at all, doesn't it? How would you go about asking for help?

The bossy *gallito* goes from friend to friend, frantically asking each one to help him clean his beak so he can go to his uncle's wedding. But it is all to no avail. In his hurry to get his beak cleaned up, this bossy *gallito* forgets his manners. He forgets to be courteous. Soon he begins to order all his friends around. One by one they stand up to him, until finally he finds the one friend who knows him well, who understands him, and who is willing to help him out in his time of need.

Read *The Bossy Gallito* to learn who the bossy rooster tries to order around and who finally comes to his rescue, setting in motion a series of events that make it possible for him to get to the wedding on time—and with a clean beak, of course!

Baseball in April and Other Stories, by Gary Soto

What would you do if your school was having a talent show and you decided to show off your talents by portraying a famous singer, singing one of his or her hit songs? Would you memorize every single word and lip-sync the song's every note? What if something terrible happened in the middle of your performance? What could be the worst possible scenario? How would you respond in that situation? Remember, you're on stage. Hundreds of people are watching you. You are being taped. Smile! This is exactly the dilemma Manuel faces in the short story "La Bamba."

How many of you have a bike? How many of you like to ride bikes? Let's pretend for a moment that your favorite thing to do in the whole world is to ride your bike everywhere. I mean everywhere: to school, to the grocery store, to Tía Raquel's house, or just cruising through the neighborhood. And let's say that one day you are walking—excuse me—cruising home from school and you pass a cute gal with ponytails and straight teeth and you decide that you should be a Good Samaritan and help out her brother, who is stuck on the fence. She says thank you and smiles. You decide you definitely want to ask her out. What would you say? Would you say, "Would you like to go on a date with me?" Or would you say, "Would you like to go bike riding with me?"

Just as you are getting ready for your big date you decide you better get your bike ready. You take the chain off the bicycle because it needs to be greased. After all, you want your bike to be in tip-top shape. But suddenly—clear out of the blue—the chain breaks. Can you believe it? "This can't be happening," you say. What do you do? Do you cancel your bike date? Do you just not show up? Or do you barter with your brother to lend you his bike in exchange for something he's been wanting for some time? You'll probably have to do kitchen duty single-handedly for weeks to come. Find out how Alfonso resolves his dilemma in "Bike Chain," another short story from Gary Soto's short-story collection.

The common, everyday dilemmas that ordinary kids like you face are the subject of Gary Soto's *Baseball in April and Other Stories*. Kids everywhere have been reading and enjoying the stories in *Baseball in April* for years. It's been so popular that the publisher has been printing it for a decade! Read all eleven stories for yourself. *¡No te la piedras!* Don't miss them, or you'll miss a beat!

Activities

for the Illustrator Award Books

2006
MEDAL WINNER

Doña Flor: A Tall Tale about a Giant Woman with a Great Big Heart, **illustrated by Raúl Colón and written by Pat Mora**

ACTIVITY 1: Making Tortillas

Make tortillas with Doña Flor and sing the tortilla song. Contrast tortilla sizes using the word *tortillitas* for little tortillas and *tortillotas* for big tortillas. The tortilla song can be found in *Diez Deditos / Ten Little Fingers and Other Play Rhymes and Action Songs from Latin America*, selected by José-Luis Orozco and illustrated by Elisa Kleven (New York: Dutton Children's Books, 1997).

> ### Little Tortillas
> *Tortillitas, tortillitas, tortillitas para mamá*
> *Tortillitas, tortillitas, tortillitas para papá*
> *Las bonitas para mamá,*
> *Las quemaditas para papá.*

Reverse *bonitas* (pretty ones) and *quemaditas* (burnt ones) so that Mamá and Papá each receive a pretty one and a burnt one.
   To make big tortillas, use the word *tortillotas*.

> ### Big Tortillas
> *Tortillotas, tortillotas, tortillotas para mamá*
> *Tortillotas, tortillotas, tortillotas para papá*
> *Las grandotas para mamá*
> *Las chiquitas para papá.*

Reverse *grandotas* (big ones) and *chiquitas* (little ones) so that Mamá and Papá each receive a big tortilla and a little tortilla.

ACTIVITY 2: Let's Pretend to Float Away on a Tortilla Raft

Ask the children who have just made big tortillas if their tortillas are big enough to serve as a raft. (1) Have the children pretend they are swimming toward the raft. (2) Have them lie or sit as they would on the raft. (3) Ask them to pretend that they have a stick or an oar. Have them row as they float away on the tortilla.

ACTIVITY 3: Stretch Exercise Song or Ending Song—
"Head, Shoulders, Knees, and Toes"

Model for the children how they should touch their heads, shoulders, knees, and toes as they sing the song.

Cabeza, hombros, rodillas, y dedos,	Head, shoulders, knees, and toes,
Rodillas y dedos	Knees and toes
Cabeza, hombros, rodillas, y dedos,	Head, shoulders, knees, and toes,
Rodillas y dedos	Knees and toes
Cabeza y hombros, rodillas y dedos,	Head and shoulders, knees and toes,
Cabeza, hombros, rodillas, y dedos,	Head, shoulders, knees, and toes,
Rodillas y dedos.	Knees and toes.

ACTIVITY 4: Roar Like a Puma

Supplies needed

One paper towel tube or toilet paper tube for each child in storytime. Pass out paper towel or toilet paper tubes and ask the children to pretend their tubes are logs. Have the children roar through the tube in unison . . . Rrrr-oarrr! Now have the children roar in groups of five, with the small ones all together and the big ones all together. Now mix the groups. Ask the children if there were differences in the sounds.

HONOR

Arrorró, Mi Niño: Latino Lullabies and Gentle Games,
selected and illustrated by Lulu Delacre

ACTIVITY 1: Act Out the Motions for "Pimpón"

Form a circle and sing the song using hand motions. Ask the children to follow along as you pretend you are washing your face and hands, combing your hair, wiping away tears, and shaking hands. Open and close your fingers to show the twinkling stars. Form a pillow with your hands, "Good Night."

Pimpón es un muñeco	Pimpón is a nice puppet
con manos de cartón.	with hands made out of paper.
Se lava la carita	He likes to wash his face
con agua y con jabón.	with soap and lots of water.
Pimpón es un muñeco	Pimpón is a nice puppet
con manos de cartón.	with hands made out of paper.
Se lava las manitas	He likes to wash his hands
con agua y con jabón.	with soap and lots of water.

Se desenreda el pelo	Pimpón fixes his hair
con peine de marfil.	with a comb or with a brush.
Y aunque no le gusta,	Although he doesn't like it,
no llora, ni hace así.	he doesn't make a fuss.
Pimpón dame la mano	Pimpón shakes hands with me
con un fuerte apretón,	with a big, happy smile.
que quiero ser tu amigo	He likes to be my friend
Pimpón, Pimpón, Pimpón.	Pimpón, Pimpón, Pimpón.
Y cuando las estrellas	And when the stars are blinking
comienzan a salir,	up in the pretty sky,
Pimpón se va a la cama.	Pimpón closes his eyes,
Pimpón se va a dormir.	And he whispers, "Good night."

ACTIVITY 2: Let's Put Baby to Sleep

Pretend you are putting your doll to sleep. Rock the doll to the tune of "Arrorró, mi niño."

Arrorró, mi niño,	Hush-a-bye, my child,
Que te canto yo.	I'll sing you a song.
Arrorró, mi niño	Hush-a-bye, my child,
Que ya se durmió.	Who has fallen asleep
Este niño lindo	This beautiful child
Se quiere dormir,	Who wants to sleep
Cierra los ojitos	Closes his eyes
Y los vuelve a abrir.	And then opens them again.

ACTIVITY 3: Let's Sing Los Pollitos

Sing "Los Pollitos" from the *Arrorró, Mi Niño* collection.

Los pollitos dicen	Baby chicks are singing
"Pío, pío, pío,"	"Pío, pío, pío,"
Cuando tienen hambre,	"Mama we are hungry,"
Cuando tienen frio.	"Mama we are cold."
La gallina busca	Mama looks for wheat,
El maíz y el trigo,	Mama looks for corn,
Les da la comida	Mama feeds them dinner,
Y les presta abrigo.	Mama keeps them warm.
Bajo sus dos alas	Under mama's wings
Acurrucaditos	Sleeping in the hay
Hasta el otro día	Baby chicks all huddle
Duermen los pollitos.	Until the next day.

César: ¡Sí, Se Puede! Yes, We Can! illustrated by David Diaz and written by Carmen T. Bernier-Grand

ACTIVITY 1: Group Discussion

Have the class or group discuss issues affecting their country, community, or school. Encourage them to develop a slogan and a plan of action to create changes that will positively influence the issue.

ACTIVITY 2: Build a Better Community

As a group, develop a list of community service activities that students can engage in to create a better community. This may include cleaning up a park or vacant lot, assisting the elderly in keeping up their homes, providing health information to a targeted group, etc. Help them organize their activities so that they can see positive changes through their efforts.

ACTIVITY 3: Write a Poem

Write an acrostic poem using words beginning with the letters in César Chávez's name.

ACTIVITY 4: Make a Map

Create a map that shows significant places in the life of César Chávez. Find newspaper or magazine articles about the events that occurred in each place to help illustrate it.

ACTIVITY 5: Make a *¡Sí, Se Puede!* Flag

Supplies needed

> white construction paper
> black construction paper
> red construction paper
> glue sticks
> six-inch dowels
> pencils
> felt-tip markers (primarily black and red)

Precut five-inch circles from the white construction paper. From the black construction paper, precut a four-inch-wide version of the Aztec bird depicted on the official flag of the United Farm Workers. Have the children paste the bird onto the circle and then paste the circle onto a precut half-sheet of red construction paper. Have each child make two. Paste the two together, placing a six-inch dowel between them for a flagpole.

This activity is taken from the REFORMA website (http://www.reforma.org/CYASCSchool-ageSpanishandbilingualprogram.doc) and was developed by Oralia Garza de Cortés. For additional activities, see "Latino Culture," by Oralia Garza de Cortés, in *Venture into Cultures: A Resource Book of Multicultural Materials and Programs*, 2nd ed., edited by Olga R. Kuharets (Chicago: American Library Association, 2001).

***My Name Is Celia: The Life of Celia Cruz / Me llamo Celia: La vida de
Celia Cruz*, illustrated by Rafael López and written by Monica Brown**

ACTIVITY 1: Sing and Dance

Play a few songs from a Celia Cruz CD, such as *The Best of Celia Cruz*. (1) Take
the lead in dancing and allow the children to dance and move. Then ask them,
"How does this music make you feel?" (2) Ask the children to listen carefully to
the CD for the conga drum, the bongos, the trumpet, and Celia's voice and ask
them to identify each. If available, pass some of these instruments around for
the children to see and try themselves.

ACTIVITY 2: Let's Dance

Sing the song "Juanito/Little Johnny" as outlined by Rose Treviño: "In this
delightful song, you get to shake, jiggle, and twist different parts of your body
as you sing. Clap your hands, too! Get your whole body in motion, from head
to toe, as the song progresses" (from "Buenos Dias / Good Morning: Bilingual
Programs for Children," in *Library Services to Youth of Hispanic Heritage*, ed.
Barbara Immroth and Kathleen de la Peña McCook [Jefferson, NC: McFarland,
2000]).

Juanito cuando baila,	When little Johnny dances,
baila, baila, baila.	he dances, dances, dances.
Juanito cuando baila,	When little Johnny dances,
baila con el pie,	he dances with his foot,
con el pie, pie, pie.	with his foot, foot, foot.
Juanito cuando baila,	When little Johnny dances,
. . . la rodilla, dilla, dilla	. . . knee
. . . la cadera, dera, dera	. . . hip
. . . la mano, mano, mano	. . . hand
. . . el codo, codo, codo	. . . elbow
. . . el hombro, hombro, hombro	. . . shoulder
. . . la cabeza, eza, eza	. . . head

ACTIVITY 3: Let's Make Salsa

While playing Celia Cruz music in the background, make some salsa using the
recipe given in *25 Latino Craft Projects*, by Ana-Elba Pavon and Diana Borrega
(Chicago: American Library Association, 2003). Ask the children to think about
and discuss the similarities between salsa music and the salsa we eat.

ACTIVITY 4: Movie Time

For those in fifth grade and older, show the movie *Mad Hot Ballroom* (2005).
Discuss the movie in general and then ask how "dance" affected the lives of the
children going to school and living in the Bronx and in Queens.

2004
MEDAL WINNER

Just a Minute: A Trickster Tale and Counting Book, by Yuyi Morales

ACTIVITY 1: Create Señor Calavera

Create your own version of Señor Calavera using the skeleton pattern in *25 Latino Craft Projects*, by Ana-Elba Pavon and Diana Borrego (Chicago: American Library Association, 2003).

ACTIVITY 2: Counting Song

Count in English and Spanish, then sing the *dos y dos son cuatro* song:

Dos y dos son cuatro,	Two plus two equals four,
Cuatro y dos son seis.	Four plus two equals six.
Seis y dos son ocho,	Six plus two equals eight,
Ocho y dos son diez.	Eight plus two equals ten.

HONOR

The Pot That Juan Built, illustrated by David Diaz
and written by Nancy Andrews-Goebel

ACTIVITY 1: Clay Pot Designs

Purchase small unglazed clay pots and have the children paint them.

ACTIVITY 2: Modeling Clay Pots

Distribute modeling clay to your group and ask them to make pots. Begin by showing samples of clay pots. Provide different colors of clay for making designs.

ACTIVITY 3: Juan Quezada Sculpture

Have the children study the story of Juan Quezada as depicted in Tiburcio Soteno's sculpture *Arbol de la Vida*, pictured at http://www.mexicanceramic .com/arbol/arboljuan.htm. How do the scenes in this tree of life sculpture compare to the scenes in the book?

ACTIVITY 4: Favorite Pottery

Use an encyclopedia or art book to find pictures of pottery made by Juan Quezada and the people of Mata Ortiz, Mexico. Discuss the characteristics of the pots and have the children pick their favorites.

Harvesting Hope: The Story of César Chávez, illustrated by Yuyi Morales and written by Kathleen Krull

ACTIVITY 1: Color the Flag

Pass out black-and-white copies of the United Farm Workers flag for the children to color.

ACTIVITY 2: Trace the Protest March Route

On a map of California, have the children highlight the route of the protest march from Delano to Sacramento.

First Day in Grapes, illustrated by Robert Casilla and written by L. King Pérez

ACTIVITY 1: Vegetable Garden

Set up a chalkboard, dry-erase board, or flip-chart and provide as many different colors of chalk or markers as you can. After telling the story, have the children take turns drawing the fruits and vegetables mentioned in the book: oranges, apples, onions, tomatoes, peppers, grapes, artichokes, onions, garlic, lemons, radishes, dates, raisins, and cucumbers. Have pictures of those that might not be familiar to the children.

ACTIVITY 2: Family Stories

Chico selected a picture of a white house with bushes and flowers and wrote a story about what he saw. Distribute a variety of pictures and have your group write their own stories.

2002
MEDAL WINNER

Chato and the Party Animals, illustrated by Susan Guevara and written by Gary Soto

ACTIVITY 1: Plan a Party!

Have your group draw a banner and make invitations. Provide goody bags, a cake, and colorful decorations.

ACTIVITY 2: Party Activity

For this outdoor activity, purchase balloons and fill them with water. Give each child a chance to throw the balloons in a bucket placed about three feet away.

ACTIVITY 3: *Las Mañanitas*

Sing *Las Mañanitas*. You can play a recording of this birthday song and practice with the kids as you sing along.

ACTIVITY 4: Neighborhood Map

Have the children make maps of their neighborhoods, using the one on the page where the animals are looking for Novio Boy as a guide.

HONOR

Juan Bobo Goes to Work, illustrated by Joe Cepeda and retold by Marisa Montes

ACTIVITY 1: Similar Stories, Similar Characters

Read one or two of the following stories to the class: *Soap, Soap, Don't Forget the Soap* by Tom Birdseye (New York: Holiday House, 1993), *Epossumondas* by Coleen Salley (San Diego: Harcourt, 2002), and *Lazy Jack* by Vivian French (Cambridge, MA: Candlewick, 1995). Ask the class to discuss how these stories are similar to *Juan Bobo* and how they are different.

ACTIVITY 2: More Juan Bobo

Find other stories about Juan Bobo in the library. Choose one of the stories to tell to the class, or have the class divide into groups to act out the stories in the books.

ACTIVITY 3: Silly Juan Bobo

Ask the class to choose their favorite silly thing that Juan Bobo did and draw a picture of it.

2000
MEDAL WINNER

Magic Windows / Ventanas mágicas, by Carmen Lomas Garza

ACTIVITY 1: *Papel Picado*

Supplies needed

> tissue paper
> scissors
> string or yarn

Instructions

1. Distribute scissors and one sheet of tissue paper about the size of a sheet of construction paper.
2. Begin by folding the tissue paper in half.
3. Fold it in half three more times
4. Fold the paper over once more about one inch from the top.
5. Use the scissors to clip geometric designs on each side of the paper, but do not cut within that one inch from the top that you folded over.
6. Unfold the paper and see the shapes you have cut.
7. Repeat with a second sheet of tissue paper.

8. Place a piece of yarn lengthwise to connect both sheets in the top inch through which you did not cut.
9. Fold the top end over the yarn and glue that end.

You can string many of these sheets together to make a colorful banner.

ACTIVITY 2: Stencil Art

Create stencil art. Distribute stencils and construction paper. Then have your group trace the stencils and color in the designs.

HONOR

Barrio: José's Neighborhood, by George Ancona

ACTIVITY 1: Paint a Mural

Roll out a craft-paper roll or butcher paper and distribute crayons. Let each child be creative. You may want to show examples of murals by having books available for them to look through.

ACTIVITY 2: *Carnaval* Mask

Make a mask to celebrate *Carnaval*. Look for books on *Carnaval* for examples and ideas.

ACTIVITY 3: Murals and Latino Culture

Invite members of the community to elaborate on various aspects of the book. Topics can include the importance of murals in Latino culture, food, *Carnaval*, and the ways different cultures celebrate Day of the Dead.

Mama and Papa Have a Store, by Amelia Lau Carling

ACTIVITY 1: Mayan Yarn Paintings

Have the children do simple Mayan yarn paintings by gluing yarn to a piece of cloth. You can have them simulate the Mayan patterns in Carling's book.

ACTIVITY 2: Dim Sum Samples

Find a Chinese-Latino community resource that can provide a sort of Latino dim sum. Everyone is sure to enjoy the opportunity to taste the fusion of the two cultures' traditional foods.

ACTIVITY 3: Mini Store Display

Display some of the items mentioned in the book, such as buttons, ribbons, paper lanterns, perfume, soy sauce, and more.

ACTIVITY 4: Abacus Demonstration

Use an abacus to demonstrate addition, and describe how it was the fastest way to add until calculators were invented.

The Secret Stars, illustrated by Felipe Dávalos and written by Joseph Slate

ACTIVITY 1: Secret Stars

Have the children draw the three kings. Ask that they include secret stars in the kings' wardrobe and in the scenery around them. Provide metallic colors or glitter.

ACTIVITY 2: *Rosca de Reyes*

Call a *panaderia* (a Mexican bakery) and order a *Rosca de Reyes*, which is a Mexican sweet bread shaped like a crown. You might even ask families in your Latino community to come to the library to talk about the bread and what can be found inside it. (To avoid allergic reactions, always obtain permission from parents or guardians for participation in food-related activities.)

ACTIVITY 3: Make Bread

Teach the children to make *Rosca de Reyes*. You can find a recipe in a Mexican baked goods cookbook or online.

1998
MEDAL WINNER

Snapshots from the Wedding, illustrated by Stephanie Garcia and written by Gary Soto

ACTIVITY 1: Family Collage

Make a wedding or family collage. Use family pictures or cut pictures from magazines. Glue these onto a large poster board.

ACTIVITY 2: Shadow Box Snapshots

Let each child make a wedding or family snapshot using clay. Distribute clay, yarn, fabric, and beads, and let the group be creative. Provide shoe boxes to give a shadow-box look to the project.

ACTIVITY 3: Celebrate!

Bring clothes or fabric remnants, and have each child wear something and pretend they are part of a celebration. They can design their own attire. Have an instant camera on hand to take snapshots.

HONOR

In My Family / En mi familia, by Carmen Lomas Garza

ACTIVITY 1: Make Piñatas

Supplies needed

    small white paper bags (lunch bag size)
    crayons

candy
crepe paper streamers in assorted colors
stapler
glue
yarn
hole punch

Distribute one bag, several crayons, and four twelve-inch streamers to each child. Ask each child to decorate the bag by drawing pictures on both sides. Glue the four streamers to the bottom of the bag. Hand out candy, and have each child put some in his or her bag. Fold the top of the bag over and staple it. Punch a hole at the top of the bag, string a piece of yarn through it, and tie the bag shut with the yarn.

ACTIVITY 2: Family Pictures

Ask the children to paint pictures of special events that have happened in their families. If the group is small enough, ask each of them to share their painting with the group and describe the event. Consider having them write a few sentences describing the event and then display the paintings in the library. If you can provide the children with a large flip-chart size piece of paper, you might find that some of the artists are more inspired with a larger canvas. Temporarily hanging these large pieces of paper on the wall during the sharing portion also has the effect of converting the library into a museum.

Gathering the Sun: An Alphabet in Spanish and English, illustrated by Simón Silva and written by Alma Flor Ada

ACTIVITY 1: Repeat after Me

Read each line of "Orgullo"/"Pride" separately and have the children repeat it before you move on to the next line. Read the poem at least twice. Have the children write their own alphabet book based on their family, language, and culture.

ACTIVITY 2: Fruits, Vegetables, and Poems

Ask each child to choose a fruit or vegetable that he or she likes and to write a poem about it. Provide pictures of fruits and vegetables around the room for inspiration.

ACTIVITY 3: Sounds

Read the poem "Lluvia"/"Rain." The sounds in this poem are metaphors for musical instruments. Play a recording of rain and have the class write a poem about the sounds. Or play a recording of an orchestra and ask the class to draw a picture of what the sounds remind them of.

ACTIVITY 4: The Yucatán and the Pyramids

Have the class find the Yucatán on a map. Help them find pictures of the pyramids of Yucatán in an encyclopedia or library book.

The Golden Flower: A Taino Myth from Puerto Rico, illustrated by Enrique O. Sánchez and written by Nina Jaffe

ACTIVITY 1: The Taino People

Introduce the Taino people and their island home of Boriquén. Explain that the island is now called Puerto Rico and its people Puerto Ricans, but when it was Boriquén the people who lived there were called the Taino. Display other books about the Taino and their stories.

ACTIVITY 2: Water Spout

Discuss this retelling of how water came to pour out of a large pumpkin. Have your group draw a picture of a pumpkin with water pouring out of it. Ask them to draw the sea creatures they would find.

ACTIVITY 3: Sand Art

Experiment with sand art by inviting a presenter to work with your group to design a sand painting of the "tall mountain that stood alone on a wide desert plain."

1996
MEDAL WINNER

Chato's Kitchen, illustrated by Susan Guevara and written by Gary Soto

ACTIVITY 1: Paper Airplane Invitation

Make a paper airplane invitation. Design an invitation on an 8½-by-11-inch sheet of paper, and then fold the paper into an airplane. Distribute crayons so that the children can make the paper airplane colorful.

ACTIVITY 2: Party Foods for Chato

Bring a sample of some of Chato's dinner foods, such as tortillas and salsa. You can purchase a package of *tamarindo* drink in the Latino food sections of some grocery stores.

ACTIVITY 3: *Tortillitas*

Recite the *tortillitas* rhyme in both English and Spanish:

Tortillitas para Mamá.	Tortillitas for Mama.
Tortillitas para Papá.	Tortillitas for Papa.
Las quemaditas para Mamá.	The toasted, burnt ones for Mama.
Las bonitas para Papá.	The good little tasty ones for Papa.

ACTIVITY 4: Make a Menu

Have the children make menus for a special meal. List the main course, vegetables, soup, salad, appetizers, dessert, and refreshments. They can design their menus with attractive borders. They can also make imaginary tostadas by drawing one on a sheet of paper and adding some of Chato's favorite ingredients like *frijoles*, *carne asada*, guacamole, and salsa. A tostada is a crispy corn tortilla and can be found in a grocery store near the tortillas.

HONOR

Pablo Remembers: The Fiesta of the Day of the Dead, by George Ancona

ACTIVITY 1: Day of the Dead Altar

Have the children make their own Day of the Dead altar. This community altar for the Day of the Dead can be placed in the library. Provide the foundation for the altar and the basic items that should be included, which are listed below. Invite community members to bring their own items for the altar. Find a community member or artist to assist you if you do not have experience in making a Day of the Dead altar. You will need to provide the following:

   a table and tablecloth;
   a picture of a famous deceased person (such as a president, actor, or
      musician) to be the centerpiece of the altar;
   some favorite foods of the deceased person;
   one or more sugar skulls;
   incense or candles;
   grooming supplies such as soap and a toothbrush;
   a favorite book, CD, or both; and
   papel picado to decorate the edges of the altar.

ACTIVITY 2: Ancestors—A Family Story

Have each member of the class write a story about one of his or her ancestors. They may need to ask their parents or grandparents to tell them about the person or show them a picture.

The Bossy Gallito / El gallo de bodas: A Traditional Cuban Folktale, illustrated by Lulu Delacre and retold by Lucía M. González

ACTIVITY 1: Invitations to Tío Perico's Wedding

After reading the story, distribute blank cards and have each child design an invitation to Tío Perico's wedding. They can use their imaginations to make the cards as fancy as they would like.

ACTIVITY 2: Sequences

Have the kids repeat back to you the sequence of events that occurred when the bossy *gallito* saw the two kernels of corn. Write these on a poster board.

ACTIVITY 3: Spanish Words

Copy the list of Spanish words provided at the back of the book onto a large sheet of poster board. Pronounce each word using the pronunciation guide. Then have the class repeat each word several times, and then say the word in English.

Family Pictures / Cuadros de familia, by Carmen Lomas Garza

ACTIVITY 1: Fingerplay

Mi familia	*My Family*
Este chiquito es mi hermanito.	This tiny one is my little brother.
Esta es mi mamá.	This one is my mother.
Este altito es mi papá.	This tall one is my father.
Esta es mi hermana.	This one is my sister.
¡Y este chiquito y bonito soy YO!	And this little and pretty one is ME!

ACTIVITY 2: Sing the Piñata Song

The piñata song can be found on the CD *De Colores and Other Latin-American Folk Songs for Children*, by José-Luis Orozco (Berkeley, CA: Arcoiris Records, 1995).

Piñata	*Piñata*
Dale, dale, dale,	Strike it, strike it, strike it,
No pierdas el tino.	Don't lose your grip.
Porque si lo pierdes	Because if you lose it,
pierdes el camino.	You will lose your way.

ACTIVITY 3: Cakewalk

Have a cakewalk with cupcakes. Use masking tape to make the circle, marking off sections and numbering each of them. Give each cupcake a number. Start the music and ask the kids to start walking around the circle. When the music stops, each child receives the cupcake with the same number as the section they end up in. You can be creative and have each cupcake decorated differently. Be aware of food allergies—be sure you have permission from a parent or guardian for each child's participation.

WEB RESOURCES

Association for Library Service to Children: The Pura Belpré Award

http://www.ala.org/ala/alsc/awardsscholarships/literaryawds/belpremedal/
  belprmedal.htm

This site was developed by ALSC and includes information about the Pura Belpré Award, including present and past winners as well as the honor books.

REFORMA: 2004 Pura Belpré Award

http://www.reforma.org/belpreaward.html

REFORMA, the Association to Promote Library Service to Latinos and the Spanish Speaking, has developed this site, which has a link to the ALSC page on the award as well as links to the home pages of some of the award-winning authors and illustrators.

Alma Flor Ada

http://www.almaflorada.com

Alma Flor Ada says, "My greatest joy is writing for children and the happiness of seeing my books in the hands of young children, and of the many children in my family." Her website includes photos, letters, and printable coloring pages.

Francisco X. Alarcón

http://www.sagepage.org/artists/francisco_x_alarcon/francisco_x.htm

Francisco X. Alarcón's website is available in English and Spanish. View his site for more information about him, his poetry, and his work in schools.

Julia Alvarez

http://www.juliaalvarez.com

"Welcome!" says Julia Alvarez at her website. "Let me introduce myself. I'm a writer of novels, essays, books for young readers, [and] poetry." On her site you can find information about her books, appearances, and more.

George Ancona

http://www.eduplace.com/kids/hmr/mtai/ancona.html

This Houghton Mifflin Reading site has biographical information as well as a list of Ancona's books.

Carmen T. Bernier-Grand

http://www.hevanet.com/grand/

Carmen T.'s site references her imagination as a child and more.

Monica Brown

http://www.monicabrown.net

Learn more about Monica Brown at her website, which includes a link to her NPR interview.

Viola Canales

http://www.harvard-magazine.com/on-line/010611.html

This *Harvard Magazine* article, "The Beauty of Beans: A Mexican American Girl Grows Up," contains biographical information about Canales.

Joe Cepeda

http://www.joecepeda.com/home/home.htm

This site includes links to Cepeda's biography and a portfolio of his work.

Raúl Colón

http://www.raulcolon.com

View Colón's portfolio and read about his work on this site filled with biographical information and more.

Lulu Delacre

http://www.luludelacre.com

This site provides quick links to Delacre's biography and her public speaking schedule. A listing of Delacre's works can also be found on this site, which includes photos.

David Diaz

http://www.rif.org/art/illustrators/diaz.mspx

You can find biographical information about Diaz at this Reading Is Fundamental site as well as links to his work, including his award-winning illustrated books.

Maya Christina Gonzalez

http://www.mayagonzalez.com

Gonzalez's site features her work, her awards, and a list of her shows.

Susan Guevara

http://www.susanguevara.com

Chorizo, the dog from the Chato books by Gary Soto, is the first thing you see on Susan Guevara's website. Links below the image of Chorizo take you to more information about Guevara her work, and her speaking engagements.

Juan Felipe Herrera

http://falcon.jmu.edu/~ramseyil/herrera.htm

This site provides a biography of Herrera and lesson plans to use with his books.

Francisco Jiménez

http://www.scu.edu/fjimenez

On this site you can find study guides for *The Circuit* and *Breaking Through* as well as book reviews and a biography of Jiménez.

Carmen Lomas Garza

http://www.carmenlomasgarza.com

This link is to the official website of Carmen Lomas Garza, which describes her as "a Chicana narrative artist who creates images about the everyday events in the lives of Mexican Americans based on her memories and experiences in South Texas." Included is a guided tour of her work and research links.

Rafael López

http://www.rafaellopez.com/noticias.htm

Visit this site to view a gallery of López's work.

Marisa Montes

http://www.marisamontes.com

Sign Montes's guest book and click on "Piñata Concentration," a game based on the book *Get Ready for Gabí*.

Pat Mora

http://www.patmora.com

Visit Pat Mora's site and read all about her, her writing, and her passion for connecting children and books.

Yuyi Morales

http://www.yuyimorales.com

A playful child greets you at Yuyi Morales's website. Click on the child to enter Yuyi's world of books and more. Señor Calavera greets you, and you can download and then print a puppet and mask to decorate.

Judith Ortiz Cofer

http://www.english.uga.edu/~jcofer/home.html

This site includes several interviews with Judith Ortiz Cofer as well as her complete vita.

Pam Muñoz Ryan
http://www.pammunozryan.com

"This site is for readers. Readers who are curious about me and my books, or who want advice on how to get published, or have been assigned an author study when they'd rather be outside playing," says Pam Muñoz Ryan in the opening statement on her website. The site also includes free bookmarks to download and print.

Gary Soto
http://www.garysoto.com

At this site, you can read about Soto's numerous awards and see a list of his favorite books.

Publishers' Websites
Individual websites for the following authors and illustrators could not be located: Nancy Andrews-Goebel, Amelia Lau Carling, Robert Casilla, Felipe Dávalos, Stephanie Garcia, Lucía M. González, Nina Jaffe, Kathleen Krull, Floyd Martinez, Victor Martinez, Nancy Osa, Amada Irma Pérez, L. King Pérez, Enrique O. Sánchez, Simón Silva, and Joseph Slate. Their publishers' sites are as follows:

Arte Público Press
http://www.arte.uh.edu

Children's Book Press
http://www.childrensbookpress.org

Chronicle Books
http://www.chroniclebooks.com/site/catalog/

Dial Books for Young Readers
http://www.penguinputnam.com/static/html/aboutus/youngreaders/dial.html

G. P. Putnam's Sons
http://www.penguinputnam.com/static/html/aboutus/youngreaders/
    putnamyr.html

Harcourt
http://www.harcourtbooks.com

HarperCollins Publishers
http://www.harperchildrens.com/hch

Houghton Mifflin
http://www.houghtonmifflinbooks.com

Lee and Low Books
http://www.leeandlow.com

Marshall Cavendish
http://www.marshallcavendish.com

Northland Publishers (Luna Rising, Rising Moon)
http://www.northlandbooks.com

Random House (includes Delacorte Press, Alfred A. Knopf, and Wendy Lamb Books)
http://www.randomhouse.com/kids/

Scholastic (includes Orchard Books)
http://www.scholastic.com

Simon and Schuster Books for Young Readers (includes Atheneum Books for Young Readers)
http://www.simonsayskids.com

CONTRIBUTORS

Sandra Rios Balderrama owes her public library career to the children of the migrant camps and one-room schoolhouses in San Benito County, California. Identifying the missing voices and the places where our world stories intersect has been at the heart of her library work for more than twenty years. Rios Balderrama is a founder of the Pura Belpré Award and was named REFORMA Librarian of the Year in 2003. She was the first person to hold the position of director for the Office for Diversity at the American Library Association. Currently, she is the director of RiosBalderrama Consulting and lives in Arizona.

Oralia Garza de Cortés is Program Manager of Special Initiatives for the Los Angeles Universal Preschool Program and a leading advocate of Latino children's literature. She is a past president of REFORMA, through which she has long advocated for excellence in library services for Latino children and families. She is a cofounder of the Pura Belpré Award.

Although **Jean Hatfield** is not Latina and does not speak Spanish, she dreams that all children will be able to find Latino authors and illustrators in their libraries. She is proud to be a cofounder of the Heartland Chapter of REFORMA and to have helped to develop a partnership between REFORMA and the Mountain Plains Library Association/Nevada Library Association for their conference. She has served on the Pura Belpré Award Committee, the Batchelder Award Committee, and the ALSC Children's Notable Recordings Committee.

Born in San Francisco, California, to Salvadoran immigrants, **Ana-Elba Pavon** is a Library Manager at the San Mateo Public Library. Since graduating from the University of California at Berkeley with an MLIS in 1992, Pavon has held librarian positions in both Spanish and youth services. She has conducted various workshops on and been on panels at various conferences addressing both these areas. She also coauthored *25 Latino Craft Projects* (American Library Association, 2003). Pavon is active in her local REFORMA chapter, Bibliotecas para la Gente, as well as in National REFORMA. The 2005–2006 REFORMA president, Pavon is proud to have served on the 2004 Pura Belpré Award Committee.

Rose Zertuche Treviño is a youth services consultant in Houston, Texas, who believes that all children should be exposed to books that celebrate and respect differences and similarities in people. One of her greatest compliments came from her son Steven, who, at age 10, labeled her the "Michael Jordan of librarians." She has served on the Pura Belpré Award Committee, the REFORMA Children and Young Adult Services Committee, the Newbery Award Committee, the Texas Bluebonnet Award Committee, and the ALSC Board.

ILLUSTRATION CREDITS

Plate 1. From *Doña Flor: A Tall Tale about a Giant Woman with a Great Big Heart*, by Pat Mora, illustrated by Raúl Colón; published by Alfred A. Knopf, an imprint of Random House Children's Books.

Plate 2. From *Chato's Kitchen*, by Gary Soto, illustrated by Susan Guevara, illustrations copyright © 1995 by Susan Guevara. Used by permission of G. P. Putnam's Sons, a division of Penguin Young Readers Group, a member of Penguin Group (USA), Inc., 345 Hudson Street, New York, NY 10014. All rights reserved.

Plate 3. From *Snapshots from the Wedding*, by Gary Soto, illustrated by Stephanie Garcia, illustrations copyright © 1997 by Stephanie Garcia. Used by permission of G. P. Putnam's Sons, a division of Penguin Young Readers Group, a member of Penguin Group (USA), Inc., 345 Hudson Street, New York, NY 10014. All rights reserved.

Plate 4. Haciendo papel picado / Making Paper Cutouts, black paper cutout, 22″ × 30″, from *Magic Windows / Ventanas mágicas*. Copyright © 1999 by Carmen Lomas Garza. Reprinted with permission of the publisher, Children's Book Press, San Francisco, CA.

Plate 5. From *Just a Minute: A Trickster Tale and Counting Book*, by Yuyi Morales. Courtesy of Chronicle Books.

Plate 6. From *Chato and the Party Animals*, by Gary Soto, illustrated by Susan Guevara, illustrations copyright © 2000 by Susan Guevara. Used by permission of G. P. Putnam's Sons, a division of Penguin Young Readers Group, a member of Penguin Group (USA), Inc., 345 Hudson Street, New York, NY 10014. All rights reserved.

INDEX